BIRTH OF THE
SUPER
YOU

BIRTH OF THE SUPER YOU

*Knowing Strength, Peace and Abundance
in a Stress-Fuelled World*

A WARRIOR'S HANDBOOK
JACOB GALEA

BALBOA.
PRESS
A DIVISION OF HAY HOUSE

Edited by Leela J. Williams
Cover Design by Robert Rulli
Typeset by Bookhouse, Sydney

Balboa Press books may be ordered through booksellers or by contacting:

Balboa Press
A Division of Hay House
1663 Liberty Drive
Bloomington, IN 47403
www.balboapress.com.au
1 (877) 407-4847

Because of the dynamic nature of the Internet, any web addresses or links contained in this book may have changed since publication and may no longer be valid. The views expressed in this work are solely those of the author and do not necessarily reflect the views of the publisher, and the publisher hereby disclaims any responsibility for them.

The author of this book does not dispense medical advice or prescribe the use of any technique as a form of treatment for physical, emotional, or medical problems without the advice of a physician, either directly or indirectly. The intent of the author is only to offer information of a general nature to help you in your quest for emotional and spiritual well-being. In the event you use any of the information in this book for yourself, which is your constitutional right, the author and the publisher assume no responsibility for your actions.

Any people depicted in stock imagery provided by Thinkstock are models, and such images are being used for illustrative purposes only. Certain stock imagery © Thinkstock.

Printed in the United States of America.

ISBN: 978-1-4525-2535-8 (sc)
ISBN: 978-1-4525-2536-5 (e)

Balboa Press rev. date: 08/22/2014

To my two angels, may this book guide you to live with great health, abundance and happiness as the best version of yourselves possible. Your inner warrior is waiting to serve you and guide you to your truth and a life of peace. All my love, from my soul – JG

Acknowledgements

My gratitude is with everyone who has supported me through the birth of this book.

Thank you to Leon Nacson and Leela Williams, to MJ Bale for sponsoring me, to all the masters and martial artists who have shared their wisdom and knowledge with me, to all of my mentors along the way, to my family and friends for their ongoing support and belief in me, to my brother who is the strongest warrior I know, and to all of my clients who have explored the depths of their souls with me.

Contents

Editor's Note

People can present differently in real life to the character they portray in polished text. After more than fifteen years of editing, I still find it interesting to speak with an author after reading their printed work. I was intrigued by the passion, energy and sincerity of Jacob's manuscript, but what made it outstanding was that it wasn't sensational. By that, I mean he was not making exclusive claims to a new and revolutionary solve-all technique that was the only true path to a richer life. The manuscript was not offering a quick fix nor was it a glorified sales brochure directing the reader to his courses or life coaching sessions. His draft was more than idealised promises, it was practical, hands-on advice that would endure the lows as well as the highs that life is bound to spring on even the most positive, enlightened people on the planet. I was curious as to whether the paper character would match the reality of the writer. I mean, when was the last time you met a success coach with humility? This author was so humble, there was barely a mention of him throughout the entire book.

My first question to Jacob was, "Where are *you* in this book?" Jacob told me he didn't want the book to be about him, he wanted it to be about the reader. Of course, a book is a journey that the author and the reader take together. I wanted to know, how Jacob knew the information he was presenting worked. How could you, the reader, trust that he wasn't sprouting off second-hand data or romanticised pop-psychology, if he didn't share his story? I loved the warrior archetype, but Jacob needed to be present in the text so that you (the reader) and I (the editor) could trust in his process.

Writing a book is a huge undertaking. When someone puts their heart and soul down on paper, they are not usually too keen on being critiqued. I basically told Jacob to get back to the drawing board but he was undaunted. On the contrary, he was gracious and listened intently to my suggestions without making excuse or argument. In that first discussion, Jacob proved himself to be an affirmative, passionate, living example of the message in his manuscript. He was committed to sharing the wisdom of warrior and if that meant reworking his draft, so be it.

Within a few weeks his story was coming to life. It was simple, and again un-sensational, but I couldn't wait for each new chapter to arrive. Jacob's approach to the obstacles and adventures of life is where the magic is. The world has not offered Jacob any special treatment, favour, tragedy or revelation. He caught a glimpse of something extraordinary within and set himself the task of exploring and understanding how it works in the ordinary world. Jacob's story encourages the belief that this 'extra' is accessible to everyone.

Jacob's manuscript landed on my desktop at a time when I could put my inner warrior to the test. I found the process lived up to its promises. For Jacob, this book has always been about you, the reader. I hope that my editorial touch has preserved his sincerity and energy so that you too can experience the wonder of the warrior within.

Leela Williams

Introduction

If you could have any super power, what would it be? Being able to fly or to breathe under water would have some pretty cool benefits. But, would your super power help you to know peace, strength and courage in this stress-fuelled world? Would it help you make dramatic changes to your everyday life? Could it get you a promotion or enhance your relationships? Do you think it would improve your decision making or encourage you to trust your instincts? Would it give you the confidence to be the hero of your life story?

Having x-ray vision won't help you sleep at night. The power to become invisible would be handy, but would it give you the conviction to pursue the life of your dreams? Would being able to time travel stop you from over-thinking decisions or would your second guessing undo the fabric of the universe before lunchtime?

Confidence, strength and peace do not come from having special powers. Nor is happiness the domain of a mythical lucky few. The capacity for real satisfaction in this world is open to everyone. The opportunity to know such fulfilment is open to you right now.

When you turn on to any form of media, you are bound to find something super. Whether it is a super hero, a super investment strategy or a super food from the super store, it is impossible to venture into the market place without finding something super. Research teams remain as committed to discovering the super qualities in our skin care products and motor oils as the marketing companies are to linking this word to absolutely anything and everything at any opportunity.

Let's face it, why would you buy juice when you can have super juice? Who would choose high-speed internet when you could have super high-speed internet? There is super cheap, super-size, the supernatural, a super ego, superannuation, super league and still the super keeps on coming! Marketing experts don't keep flogging the same message because they are lazy and unimaginative. On the contrary, they know the power of this word and they use it because it continues to work.

Effective marketing taps into what we really want. You need a car, but those slick automobile advertisements are selling you more than that. Your needs can be set out in bullet points such as fuel efficiency, reliability and safety. However, buying a car is an emotional process and however stringent our lists and budget may be, our purchasing decision is often swayed by the lifestyle assurances inherent in the marketing. When it comes to features and benefits a new car is a new car is a new car … in that they all get you from A to B. Often, what we end up buying into is a promise of prestige, freedom, control, fun, security, or a relaxing family journey without a single fight in the back seat or a disagreement over directions in the front.

The 'super' strategy works so well because of the allusion that a product or service will bring you closer to your own super qualities. Starting each morning with a breakfast of super berries, super-probiotic-super-good-for-you yoghurt and a super workout will make you feel fitter and healthier but does it make YOU super?

Many people have had a glimpse of or felt a ripple of their true potential. You might not dare to admit that a super version of you exists, not even to yourself. However, the fact that you have picked up this book means you at least suspect there is more to you and more to life. You might call it latent potential. Perhaps you feel that life dealt you the wrong cards or that you never got your chance to shine. However you frame it, simply recognising that you could be more is the perfect starting place for this journey. From here, it is not a great stretch to see your hidden or untapped possibilities. You might not believe there is a *Super You* and, right now, you don't need to. If you can believe that there is just one tiny kernel of strength or a single grain of courage lying dormant within you, then this book will help you nurture that seed until being super is not just possible – it is who you are.

The 'super' marketing is making a promise it can't keep because it is impossible to awaken the *Super You* from the outside. Being super comes from the inside out, not the other way around. The biggest house on the block and a great new promotion can make you feel super for a little while, but the super feeling won't endure. Before long you will be looking for new ways to replicate the feelings that the successes of life brings. Awakening the *Super You* means that you will no longer crave the sweet treats that bring you short, sharp bouts of fulfilment. Rather you will strive towards enduring emotional and material success.

This book is testimony to the wonder, peace and strength that unlocking the *Super You* will bring. There is a super being within all of us. It is simply a matter of feeding and nurturing it. Once your inner hero or heroine is strong enough, there will be no holding them back.

This world is starved for heroes. I read an article in the paper recently that hailed Joey, a young shop attendant, as a hero. When a $20 bill dropped from the pocket of a blind man, a lady customer picked it up and pocketed it. Joey requested the money be returned to its rightful owner. When this appeal was refused, he asked the lady to leave the store as he would not serve someone so disrespectful. He then gave the blind man $20 from his own funds.

This young man stood up and did the right thing. However, we must ask ourselves why his story made the news. Joey did not feel heroic, he said he just did what he thought anyone would do but this is news because not everyone is so sure about that. Would anyone have done the same thing? Would you?

This book will introduce you to the warrior within. This is an aspect of yourself that you can count on in times of stress and through any challenge. Through the process of connecting to and awakening your inner warrior, you will encounter and merge with the very best version of yourself possible. You are going to love it. Once you meet the potential you, even for a moment, there is no going back to the mundane world. Knowing your super self and discovering your warrior's toolkit will enable you to make great changes to your world and be the hero of your journey.

You wouldn't choose fuel when you can have super fuel. You wouldn't choose an everyday life when you can have a super one. You can choose the ordinary journey or you can take the path of the

Super You. It is your choice to make. But ask yourself, why would you choose NOT to be super? Why wouldn't you take the super journey? You don't have to choose now. However, I do ask that you make the decision to be open to the idea that there is something more inside you ... something super.

Dive deep into the words of this book. Take the journey at your own pace and allow your subjective mind to absorb all the nutrients it needs to enrich the kernel of greatness within you. Awakening your super self does not mean rejecting any part of who you are now. There is nothing wrong with who you are right now. I did not create this book to belittle who are you, but as an invitation to grow into the person you were born to be. This is a process of delving beyond years of conditioning and programming so that you can assimilate all of your potential into a whole, healthy and highly effective psyche.

The *Super You* is no more and no less than the very best version of you possible. Step by step, this book will help you to become *Super You.* So be prepared for an incredible journey as you don your cape and soar into a super life that will be a legacy to all who follow.

Part One

The Warrior's Journey: Birth of the Super Self //

Chapter One **//** # Finding Warrior

You are about to awaken the warrior I know is within you.
And I am not afraid.

L et's begin by breaking the connection between the word 'warrior' and any sensationalised, rage-fuelled, revenge-powered, glory-driven imagery that may exist in your mind. The silver screen spills its glamour over everything, including its depiction of warrior.

I am unafraid to awaken this aspect in you because I know the warrior within all of us is gentle, compassionate, assertive, self-possessed, humble and empowered. A warrior is an effective and respected individual who has a strong vision for the future and plans for success. A warrior overcomes challenges, is open to new information, builds strong alliances and perseveres. A warrior accepts that every path has its trials and is prepared to meet obstacles head on with strong purpose and diligence. A warrior is responsible to themselves and has a duty of care to others. Unleashing the warrior in you is akin to inviting you to be YOU at your very best – without excuses.

|| *'The key to being a warrior is not to be afraid of who you are.'* ||

Tom Spanbauer, In the City of Shy Hunters.

I first encountered my inner warrior when I was sixteen. Before that time, I had no real need for warrior. I was young, innocent, had a girlfriend and had followed in the footsteps of my dad by taking up an apprenticeship. I had my whole life ahead of me and everything was roses.

Even in the cold and dark of 5:30 am, as I stepped off the train onto Redfern Station, my world was rosy. That this was one of the roughest train stations in Sydney had escaped my notice. I was not much more than the shy, but enthusiastic, school boy who had started his apprenticeship three months ago. I hadn't consciously noticed anything out of the ordinary. However, something must have been amiss because my subconscious was screaming at me! The knots in my stomach were trying to signal something to me, but naively, I thought it was to do with something I ate or something I didn't eat. After all, I was a growing, teenage boy and signals from my stomach were predominantly food-related. However, the feeling was not to be ignored and became louder and stronger as I walked off the platform and into a side street towards the bus stop.

In the side street I was quickly cornered by three men. They demanded my wallet, watch and phone. My system went into panic. My mouth became dry, my heart was beating out of my chest and it seemed as if everything was running in slow motion. I had no idea what to do or how to calm the panicky feeling within me. The rose-tinted glasses were off, and I was acutely aware of my surroundings.

One of the men hit me and the others laughed. I felt like an ant set upon by giants. The smell of the alcohol that had given bravado to my tormentors only fuelled my fear. Adrenalin rushed through me and my fight-or-flight response kicked in.

Instinctively, I struck out at one of the men and ran. If I was surprised that my strike could have momentarily distracted my assailants, I was stunned at my new-found speed. I ran so fast, I swear I had super powers. In those moments nothing could have stopped me from running, and run I did—straight onto the bus I had to catch to Alexandria.

As soon as I arrived at work I ran straight to the bathroom and vomited. I had never felt anything like this before. It was a crazy rush of emotions—inner turmoil, confusion, sickness and anger.

I couldn't stop thinking about what had happened all day. I told one of the men I looked up to at work. He said I should learn karate. His brother Alex, who also worked with us, just happened to be a master. The way I saw the world was again challenged. Alex was such a humble man; I would never have guessed he was dangerous, martial arts weapon!

What a day! This was my initiation into the world of the warrior. The attack in the alleyway had pushed me out of my comfort zone and forced me to re-evaluate my place in the world. I had experienced panic, fight-or-flight, adrenalin, and felt overwhelmed by a contradiction of emotion. I did not like feeling out of control. At work I didn't try to bottle up or hide my reaction to the experience.

Looking back, without that terrifying encounter, I may have completed my apprenticeship never realising I was working alongside a Master of Karate. This event was the catalyst to my taking the first step in my warrior journey. I could have gone another decade, another half a century, without having a similar wake-up call. Those three drunks literally gave me a kick-start to discovering who I am and what really makes my heart sing.

Connecting with the warrior within you will take you out of your comfort zone. I am not asking you to put your life in danger or take unnecessary risks, but it is hard to challenge your beliefs without stepping outside your familiar routine. Maybe you have already experienced the warrior within; perhaps that is why you were drawn to this book.

When life shakes us out of our comfort zones we can waste a lot of time trying to undo what has happened and return to a past that is no longer accommodating. The warrior does not try to reclaim the sleepy world of comfort. Awakened to this new reality, the warrior equips themselves with the awareness and skills required to navigate the adventure of a bigger, fuller existence.

Are you ready to awaken a brave new you?

Every journey starts with a single step and that first step can be the hardest to take. The second step is fuelled by the motion of the first, the third by the energy of the first and second, and your hundredth step championed by the ninety-ninth and so forth. The momentum of all the steps you have taken so far can make it hard for you to stop still in your tracks. However, stop still you must if you are to begin a fresh journey.

Wherever you may be on the journey of life you are at a crossroads. You will not be aware of all the options available to you until you put on the brakes and look around. There is little point rushing onto a new path until you have identified where you want to end up. As a warrior you will walk your path with dignity, determination and integrity.

Right now you are a novice. As a novice you have made mistakes. You have allowed the world to define you. As a warrior you will define yourself and influence the world around you. As a warrior you have no need for any shame, regret or frustration over past events. Everything that has happened to you as a novice will become part of your warrior's toolkit.

Plan a day for your initiation into warrior. Allow yourself at least one week to prepare for this event. Choose a day where you are free from all other obligations. Ideally, this would be first thing in the morning and you will have a whole day to celebrate the brave new you.

Prepare yourself by reflecting on your current place in the world. Give yourself a life review. Remember, until now you have been a novice. Look back at challenges in your life without judgement. Write down what you want to change about yourself. Write definitely and defiantly. If you want to be happier ask yourself what it is you really want to let go of. Is it sadness? Is it a lack of self-worth? If you want a new career, again, ask what you really want to let go of. Is it insecurity? Is it a fear of failure? Get to the core of your goals and identify your negative motivators.

By identifying any negative motivators you are able to create much stronger foundations for your goals. As warrior you must be aware of these aspects of yourself so you can transform them into something else. If you become aware of an aspect of your psyche that will not serve you or your loved ones, as a warrior, you will see it honestly, so that you may heal it and transform it into energy that will serve your purpose. A warrior will not push away or deny those parts of their self as this only makes those aspects stronger.

Once you have identified all the aspects or negative motivators you would like to let go of write them down and look at them objectively. Think of all the energy you have poured into nurturing the traits you want to be free of.

When we try to let go of an ineffective trait it leaves a gap in our psyche. Think of your mind as an intricate machine. The old-fashioned image of turning cogs works well. If a few cogs are rusting or worn and are slowing things down or putting things off track and you remove those ineffective parts, the whole process will come to a standstill. In the same way, if you focus on removing something from your life your psyche will desperately try to fill that space so the inner wheels can keep turning. You do not want your subconscious in charge of your replacement parts!

We are often encouraged to work smarter not harder. Have you heard the term 'you don't have to reinvent the wheel'? Well, it is actually smarter to work with the wheels you already have. It is easier and more energy-efficient to transform your rusty, old, dysfunctional traits into shiny, new, effective ones.

Take a look at your list. How much energy has gone into building those traits? For example, if you want to let go of fear consider how strong that fear has been in your life. How big an obstacle has it been? Look at how it has held you back and stopped you from living and enjoying your life. Now imagine all that fear working for you instead of against you.

Make a strong and conscious choice of what you are going to transform your ineffective traits into:

• Self-loathing can become self-loving;
• Poverty consciousness can become wealth awareness;

- Loneliness can be converted into autonomy;
- The novice will be transformed into the warrior.

You should now have two lists: one of the aspects that are moving out of your life, and another of all the wonderful traits of your warrior self. On the day of your initiation you will need your two lists. How elaborate you make your initiation is up to you. You might want to take your oath in front of the bathroom mirror, or you might want to yell it off a mountain top.

Begin with deep, slow breaths. Do not rush. Just breathe until you feel still and at ease. Continue to breathe slowly and deeply, and come back to that stillness as needed.

Take your first list in your hand and renounce those aspects and negative motivators. Say your goodbyes to fear, loneliness, etc.

Say out loud:

Fear no longer serves me, and I no longer serve fear.

Repeat this for each of the aspects on your list. When you are at the end of your first list, breathe again. Feel still, feel sure and feel certain. You have let go of *novice* and are about to step into *warrior*.

Make your first statement with clarity and purpose:

I am Warrior.
I am Honest.
I am Courage.

Repeat the 'I am ...' statement for all the aspects on your second list. Hold your words in your mind. Breathe them in deeply. Hold them and release them out to the universe. Allow this visualisation to expand with each breath out until it is so big it covers the entire planet. Continue to breathe deeply in and out until your breath of intention overflows into the galaxy and beyond. In this expansion your soul will recognise its limitless potential.

Observe and remember that you are limitless. Take your time in this space and listen to your inner intelligence. See and know the warrior within you. What is he/she saying to you? What can you feel? What do you see? While in this meditation do not analyse, simply observe the feelings and symbols as they arise.

When you are ready open your eyes and write down as much as you can about your experience. Try to capture what your inner voice was saying to you in a way you are comfortable with – write a detailed account, make bullet points or draw images. This output is part of your warrior pledge. Keep it with your second list, where you can readily refer to it any time you need to reconnect to your warrior spirit.

Now you have committed yourself to walk the path of the warrior. You are no longer living with the limitations you knew as a novice. You can now see the walls that limited you no longer exist. In fact, they never existed! If you doubt this affirm:

I am Warrior. I am Limitless.

It is time to cement your commitment with affirmative action. Go and do something that scares you. Tackle a task you have put off for too long; write up your resumé or apply for that job; call someone up and be honest about what has been on your mind (remembering that warrior is gentle and compassionate).

Congratulations! You have awakened the warrior within. By stepping from novice to warrior you will change your reality. The actions, words, thoughts, emotions and attitudes of the warrior will create new dynamics and opportunities all around you.

I am sure the brave new you is ready to live with courage and to pursue your passions, dreams and desires. We stand at the beginning of your journey. In the next chapter we take the first real step into your new world.

Maybe the 16-year-old novice who walked into that dark alley was granted a blessing; although this does not sanction the actions of the three assailants. With a change of perspective we see this not as the victimisation of a youth, but the awakening of a warrior.

In this world you make no mistakes. The warrior views everything life presents equally. There is no good and bad. Every challenge makes you stronger. Every obstacle you meet brings you wisdom. Life is about learning, growing, exploring, loving, laughing, crying and celebrating all the emotions you encounter; they help guide you to become the person you were put on this planet to be.

Chapter Two **//** # Stepping into Warrior

The inner warrior can be a source of limitless potential, pathways and that which may be perceived as miraculous. Now you have invoked your inner warrior it is important to remain aware of its presence and to nourish that aspect of yourself wisely.

Those men in the side street were agents of change. Through that one experience my mind was suddenly opened to so many things. I had discovered the panic of fear and the rush of adrenalin, but that was nothing compared to the mind mania that followed. I went over and over the events in my head, reliving them again and again, imagining what I should have, could have, would have done if I was bigger, stronger, faster … or simply knew they were there. Then I thought: *Now, I am going to learn how to fight. Next time things will be very, very different. If ever I meet those guys again they had better look out.*

I clearly remember walking into the karate dojo for the first time. There was a group of people dressed in white outfits with different coloured belts tied around their waists. As I walked in they all smiled and I felt so welcome. The dojo had a feeling of security and comfort about it. There was no swaggering, boasting or shows of bravado. For a place where people came to fight it was surprisingly serene, even spiritual. To me it felt absolutely perfect.

The master instructor invited me into the class. I joined the other students who were kicking and punching the air through their warm-up drills. During that class something stirred inside me. I recognised it from my encounter with the three men. When I struck out and ran to the train station it had felt like having super powers. I was threatened, panicked and, somehow, had connected to a primitive instinct. I felt frenzied and out of control. Now, I was focused and supported. I was connecting to my inner strength by choice. I felt calm and in control.

> *'I know what I'm capable of;*
> *I am a soldier now, a warrior.*
> *I am someone to fear, not hunt.'*

Pittacus Lore, The Rise of Nine

Over the next few years I trained five days a week and sometimes took two classes a night. I immersed myself in this practice. There was so much more to martial arts than I could have imagined when I stepped into that first class. It made me feel amazing. The physical training was just one aspect of what the teachers passed onto the students. The attitude I took into the first class stayed with me.

I listened, watched and absorbed everything I could from each of my teachers as well as my classmates.

Alongside physical strength I gained mental and spiritual fortitude. The funny thing was that outside of grading and tournaments I never had to use my new-found fighting skills. Once you learn something as powerful as martial arts the bad guys know. I never got picked on again. Over the years, I developed what I now know as the 'heart of a warrior'. Whether I was in a corporate boardroom or on the wrong side of town, the bad guys could sense it. Of course, my karate ability had no relevance in the business world, but a warrior is focused, self-aware and confident of his place in the world – auspicious qualities whatever the setting.

Even if I was to face a troubled situation I knew I couldn't use my skills as I might seriously injure someone. As a warrior I was powerful, confident and connected. I learnt to be aware of myself as well as my surroundings and to innately avoid or diffuse bad situations well before a punch was ever thrown. My master taught me that a wise warrior knows when to walk away. Knowing how to fight, and choosing not to, is where real strength lies.

Three years after my first class I was graded as a brown belt. At that time I recognised that I was committed to the warrior's journey. I saw this as a quest for inner excellence, strength, truth and a power so great it could move the universe. I made it my mission to help others find and connect with the warrior I know lies in us all.

In those first three years of training I knew I was in the right place. Any time I needed advice I could find it. All of the teachers carried themselves with quiet confidence and held their art in utmost respect. Diligence and integrity were at the foundations of the dojo. In this environment of camaraderie and mutual respect everyone could aspire to personal greatness. All that was required was a willingness to learn and a lot of hard work. The smiles and warmth that welcomed me into that first class were open to every student.

It is important to choose your peers wisely. I know how lucky I was to have found an environment so conducive to my personal development. You have now made the conscious decision to connect with your inner strength, but you do not need to rely on luck to provide the perfect environment for your journey. The universe has already provided you with the perfect classroom filled with incredible teachers. It is called life.

As a warrior you are always open to learning. You are the perpetual student who can learn from everyone in any situation. You are flexible in your approach and sure of your goals. You are aware of your environment, quick to assess a situation and slow to judge. You choose your peers wisely. You nourish your mind and soul with wisdom and knowledge.

Always be learning. You will be drawn to teachers for many reasons. It is most important in your early days of warriorhood that you choose your mentors wisely. Look not only at their words or the promises on their marketing brochures, but at their actions. Observe the people that surround a teacher as they are, perhaps, the best measure of what they are truly teaching. If you go into a painting class and you find the students resentful of each other's talents, this is a reflection on the teacher. If you go into a karate class and the students get involved in brawls or goad each other into fights, this too is a reflection on the teacher. Before you sign up to a class look around and do your homework.

There are many misconceptions about what makes a person strong. One of the biggest is that suffering leads to strength. In this philosophy, someone who criticises is teaching humility, someone who pushes you down is revealing your weakness, and someone who withholds advice and guidance is teaching autonomy. Too often, people mistake these kinds of abuses as being for their own good. I do not hold with these practices as in my experience you can find everything you need to grow strong, balanced and wise in a safe and compassionate environment. You do not need to suffer for your wisdom. A true warrior is truly powerful, but would never use that power to belittle another. Power is nothing outside that which it is used for.

You may be familiar with another version of the following. Its origins are often accredited to the Native Americans, but I believe it was first published by a minister in the 1970s. Whatever its roots the message remains the same.

> *'AN ESKIMO FISHERMAN came to town every Saturday afternoon. He always brought his two dogs with him. One was white and the other was black. He had taught them to fight on command and they were well matched. Every Saturday afternoon in the town square, the people would gather and these two dogs would fight and the fisherman would take bets. Some days the black dog would win and on others the white dog would win – but the fisherman always won! His friends asked him how he always knew the outcome of the fight. He said, "I starve one and feed the other. The one I feed always wins because he is stronger."'*

Imagine there are two combatants inside you. Both are powerful, strong and clever. One seeks power over others, the other seeks self-empowerment. Either of these warriors has the potential to overcome the other. Choose the one you wish to prevail and feed it well.

One of those warriors will thrive with friendships, honesty, compassion and love. The other will grow with jealousy, deception, selfishness and anger. The one you feed will become your constant companion.

You will meet many travellers on your journey. Seek out people who are self-aware and able to express themselves clearly, or at least willing to give it a try! Of course, it is ideal to surround yourself with positive people, but what exactly does that mean? A positive person could be in a real mess in the real world. They may be struggling through a mountain of challenges. Everyone can smile when things are on their side. The value of a person will come out in the tough times. So do not judge someone by their successes in life. A positive person will experience crises the same as everyone else. It is how they respond to life that makes them stand out as someone you want in your world.

Seek out people who do not get stuck blaming everyone else for their problems or expect someone else to turn up and fix things up for them. Effective personalities know that life can throw a curve ball without bias and be able to take responsibility for their part in their dramas as well as for the solutions. They also accept that good things take time and the very best things in life are worth working for.

Hypnotists know that your subconscious cannot tell the difference between a lie and a truth. Everything you see and hear is fed to your subconscious. The images in computer games, films and magazines are all valid input for your subconscious. So be conscious of what you are feeding your subconscious. When choosing a book, film or company, put positive action over violence, laughter over fear, and love over anger.

Again, the universe has already provided you with the perfect classroom filled with incredible teachers, but it is largely your choice how, when, what and from whom you learn. When the going gets tough the warrior who instinctively falls back on honesty, respect and passion will find their way.

Expect the warrior to be present in your daily affairs with wise counsel, awareness of your inner and outer environments, and a readiness to take affirmative action.

Your inner warrior also needs regular R and R, meaning time-out to recharge and reconnect. How you refresh your spiritual batteries is up to you. There is no one-size-fits-all approach to relaxation so you need to find your own method. Some people take a long silent walk, others swim and some garden. Yoga can also be effective. In essence, each of these approaches is meditative.

Meditation or periods of silence are my preference. By quietening the mind, stepping back from mental chatter and observing rather than connecting to your thoughts, you increase awareness of the self which exists outside your mental processes. You will be amazed at the solutions and clarity available to you when you turn down the static noise that dulls intellect and intuition.

The method you choose is not as important as how often you choose to engage in it. Create a regular space in your timetable to engross yourself in your meditative activity. Start on a weekly basis and build up to a more regular routine until you can commit to a daily practice. If you can establish a routine at the same time each day, even better. Some people benefit from starting the day with a brisk, meditative walk, others feel more reflective towards bed time, and your ideal time of day could come anywhere in between. Be mindful of your energy levels over any twenty-four-hour period to identify when you will most benefit from taking time out to reflect and recharge. This will become an important time for you to connect to and communicate with your inner warrior. Discipline and repetition is vital to this process.

Remember, when you shine people will see your light. Don't be a walking flat battery. Plug in, recharge and refocus the deep power that lies within you every day. There is no use having the radio on if you cannot hear the words, and there is no use asking for inner guidance if you don't stop to listen.

I suggest you now close your eyes and spend the next fifteen minutes focused on nothing but your breath and the spaces in between. This is a magical exercise that should never be underestimated. Any time you feel stressed, worried, or need to focus, simply dive back into this exercise to return to your place of silence so you can hear again.

Chapter Three **//** From Initiate to
Initiator

Becoming a brown belt can be likened to starting high school because you move into a new stage of training where you are once again at the lowest grade. The people I was now training with had shown an ongoing commitment to the karate program. Girls, parties, mates, work, study or other obligations could easily keep someone from their karate training. My new peers had not only met the physical and mental challenges of the training, but they had stayed focused despite the obstacles or distractions life had thrown them.

When I spoke to the black belts in my dojo I found that they had more than karate in common. Each of them was also successful in the world beyond martial arts. Even as a brown belt I could recognise how martial arts had changed me. I was more focused, conscious of my actions and aware of my surroundings.

These changes manifested in subtle ways in my everyday life. My interest in martial arts gave me something positive to talk about. Friends and family showed an interest in my progress and would ask about it at gatherings. So I was naturally brought into conversation and this strengthened my connection to the people around me. People were also interested in what I had to say about other areas. They were keen to give me tips, show me support, give me direction, invite me out on their boats and make me job offers.

My father, a factory worker and fitter and turner, believed that getting an apprenticeship and trade would give me a job for life. This formula worked for him, and he stuck at his trade in his factory position for security, for love, for his family and all of the other usual reasons. It had given him everything he needed, and he was convinced a good trade and a factory job was the pathway to security and happiness for me too. But it wasn't what I wanted to do.

By the time I was twenty-one, like many young adults, I wanted to be my own person. I wanted to break free of the expectation that I would follow the path my father had set out for me. There was nothing wrong with what he wanted for me, it just wasn't what I wanted for me. My dad was a practical guy and a hard worker who always put his family before his own dreams and desires. He rarely had relaxation time to himself. He was committed to raising his family and looked at his work as the platform that provided for us. His intentions for me were pure. However, there came a time when I had to release myself from the expectations that dictated what I must do for a secure and happy life. By the time I gained my brown belt I was already well on the way to breaking free of that conditioning.

Conditioning is a very powerful thing. It is powerful enough to keep an elephant from breaking free from its chains. It can hold people in relationships, jobs and anxiety, and in a mental jail if that is what they are accustomed to living in. Conditioning keeps the ordinary person from becoming extraordinary.

From very early childhood you have been learning to adapt to your world. You have developed rules and regulations that help you avoid pain, achieve pleasure and even keep you alive. For example, a child that is admonished for having an opinion learns to keep their thoughts to themselves. In more extreme cases, a child who is beaten for having an opinion may learn it is best not to have one.

Praise is also a form of conditioning. Being praised or rewarded for putting the needs of your family or workplace above your own, is also a form of conditioning. A teacher, boss, corporation or spiritual advisor may consciously or inadvertently create, contribute to, or reinforce conditioning.

How we view our place in the world, our talents and our worth, is subject to conditioning. Once a rule or belief is set it can be hard to erase. The longer a rule exists the more deeply it is etched into your subconscious mind. The conditioning that served you well in one situation can be your downfall in another. It is important not to judge conditioning in the black and white sense of positive and negative. Viewing conditioning in terms of habits that are working for you and habits that no longer serve you is far more beneficial. You can then, literally, change your mind set in the same way as you would break a bad habit. First, you have to admit to having the habit, then you need to focus on letting it go and replacing it with a more beneficial approach.

As a martial arts student I learnt to drop everything I had ever learnt. This can be likened to emptying your cup so it can be completely re-filled. The sensei (master) never set limitations with our martial arts training. He simply allowed the truth to unfold in each student as part of their unique journey. I clearly remember the training session that helped me and the other students break our conditioning.

When Sensei told us we would be breaking a wooden board with our hands, like most people, we did not believe it was possible. Our master saw it differently. He told us, not that we could, but that we *would* break the board. There was no other way.

I had seen this stunt on television demonstrations, but part of me always thought it was some kind of trick. When Sensei gave a demonstration we saw that they were real wooden boards and he broke them with his hand. It was no trick. Not only that, Sensei said we would do it too.

In turn, each of us approached the board, focused, cleared our mind and struck intent on 'the break'. Regardless of age, stature or gender, each and every student who approached the board broke it. Each of us broke through the barriers of conditioning that day. We did what we thought was, just moments before, impossible.

As a warrior your only limits are those you set upon yourself. Yes, we have all been brought up with limitations, but the sensei of life wants you to break through this with all of your strength and intention. There comes a time in all our lives where we simply have to de-clutter our minds and be free, clear and effortless. This is what the compassionate warrior is all about!

I had reached one of those times in my life; I was determined to break through the limitations and see where life could take me. Through martial arts training I had developed a cape of courage and I wore it every day. With this courage came a need for honesty and I demanded this of myself. I strove to think, act, and be as true to my character as possible. Staying in someone else's dream was not being authentic to who I had become. I wanted to break free – to be me. Simply existing day-to-day was not even an option.

Making a life change can be very hard. However, my inner warrior was impossible to deny. It wanted adventure, to take risks, to push boundaries, to live – and each day the desire grew stronger until it could no longer be ignored.

I had completed my four-year apprenticeship and was working for the number one printing company in the country. My future was securely mapped out. Most people would be content, even happy, but I wanted to follow the driving feeling within me and see where it would take me.

So I began looking around for opportunities. The idea of looking like a fool or being a failure never had a chance to shake my confidence. I was embarking on a grand adventure! I was in new territory so I accepted there would be dead ends and allowed myself some false starts. Often I had no idea what I was doing and in those times I relied on my intuition. Even when I had no idea where my inner voice was leading me to there was no way I wasn't going to obey and explore it.

Have you ever had a hunch that you didn't follow? If you have ever had a *feeling* about something, or were drawn to an opportunity, but for whatever reason didn't act on it, then you probably know how it feels to look back and wish you had taken more notice. Trusting your feelings can take you out of plan and into possibilities your logic would never acknowledge possible.

When it is time for me to sit back and reflect on my life I don't want to be wishing I had done it all differently. I want to sit back, smile, and be completely satisfied with my choices. There will be side-tracks, strange encounters and some close calls to keep me entertained, but no regrets. As you are reading this book I assume you want the same.

There is no single key that will open opportunity to you. Think of success as having multiple locks and the warrior as the combination that will free them all. Being true to yourself is an essential part of this journey. Everyone is unique and the warrior's path will be different each time it is invoked. Your view of success, your talents, your focus and your esteem will all play a part in how your future unfolds. Seek to understand each of those principles at its core. Be honest in your exploration of why you do what you do. Ask yourself how your actions and attitudes serve you and constantly look for better ways to approach your goals.

In stepping into warrior you have made a commitment to be the best person you can be. It is important to trust yourself and know that you have already everything you need to begin the process of birthing the *Super You*. This does not mean you won't need to improve your skill set or brush up on your interpersonal skills. It means that you have the essentials in your toolkit such as courage, honesty, self-worth and determination. Of this short list self-worth is the hardest to manifest.

> *"We ask ourselves, 'Who am I to be brilliant, gorgeous, talented, fabulous?' Actually, who are you not to be?"*
>
> Marianne Williamson

Affirmations can be effective in communicating to and fine-tuning your subconscious. They have become a core ingredient in most motivational programs. The most powerful affirmation is one that you create for yourself. The second list you created back in Chapter One is an example of how to craft powerful, personal affirmations. Use those 'I am' statements as your morning and evening mantra. I used an amazing affirmation when I was in the process of breaking free from the conditioning of my upbringing:

I am free, I am me, and I
trust the journey I am on.
I honour my pathway
and am proud.
I am a warrior who has an
infinite power within me.
I am that I am.

I lived and breathed this affirmation and repeated those words over and over until they were firmly etched into my subconscious. They became part of the foundations upon which I began to build my dream life. In my martial arts training I learnt the Chinese saying that the continual drip of a tap will pierce a hole through the rock. I dripped and kept on dripping onto the rock of conditioning with affirmation, powerful intention and deliberate action until it was no longer an anchor to me. Once I set myself free there was nothing that could keep me working on that printing press. There was nothing that could keep me from my destiny.

Add to your mantra as required. Be sure to use strong positive statements about who you want to be. Set them in the present and own them with the 'I am' prefix. If you want to change careers focus on the role you want to have rather than the one you are leaving behind. Letting thoughts such as, *I hate this job* or, *I am not going to work in a printing press,* dominate your thinking will keep you right where you are and may even set you a few steps backwards. Such phrases are examples of how not to create an affirmation. Effective examples include, 'I am at the top of my field', 'I am proud to be a successful entrepreneur' or, 'I love working with animals'.

Affirmations are part of the warrior's ABC where you will **A**lways **B**e **C**reating your future by **A**lways **B**eing **C**onscious of how your thoughts are supporting your intentions.

Think of your future as a white canvas; all your words, actions, thoughts and emotions are painting your upcoming masterpiece. You are the artist of your life, so create a work of art you will be proud of.

There are many benefits to keeping a diary. There is the conscious, affirmative process of putting pen to paper and setting down your vision for the future. Other benefits can come from allowing your thoughts to flow freely and pour onto the paper with as little direction or monitoring as possible.

This exercise can help you capture your emotions and words. Try this outpouring or downloading activity for a full week and then go back and read over your work. You may notice common phrases, words, concerns or attitudes you were unaware of previously. This thought diary can help you see yourself more clearly. The more clarity you have about your thoughts the more effectively you can align them with your vision.

Artists require more than a vision. They also require technique, resources and planning. Ask yourself what needs to happen to bring your dreams to fruition. What techniques and resources do you require to achieve your goals? Make a plan so that you can acquire the skills you need. Your diary is the place to record your short-term goals and map out the stepping stones to your success.

Little steps lead to big change. So don't limit yourself by becoming overwhelmed by how much you need to do. Identify what you can do and start immediately. As a warrior you are a perpetual student, and by learning from every opportunity you will progress at a quickened rate. Your diary is also a record of your progress. When you look back at your thoughts and dreams a year from now you will be surprised just how far the warrior's path has taken you.

It is now time to take the next step. I believe there are four kinds of people in this world: those who aren't ready for change, those who wish for change, those who want change and those who initiate change. The warrior sets their own path boldly. Once awakened the warrior will compel you forwards towards your goals. Trust me, the warrior does not sit around waiting for life to happen.

Chapter Four // Come Fly with Me

At any given moment in time you are at a crossroads filled with opportunities you cannot see. There is no need to be aware of all the options available to you, but you do want to hone your vision on the ones that will bring you closer to your goals.

And thus, determined to move on from my comfortable, respectable role in the printing industry, I became familiar with the careers section of the newspaper. I had no idea how things were going to come together, but I did know there was something waiting for me.

Knowing that I wanted a new career, but not knowing how to make that happen, forced me into unfamiliar waters. I had to step outside of my trade as well as the network of friends and family who had supported and guided me through my apprenticeship. I had to push myself to trust. Looking back, it is plain to see that *trusting* things would work out was more powerful than *knowing* how it would happen. If I had known how, I would not have been forced to turn to my intuition.

Listening to and acting on my intuition was a new concept for me. It was a board breaker. I had to step up to my intuition with intent and focus and go for it! Once I did this, the newspaper with its uninspiring careers section, suddenly had the answer I was looking for; in fact, the newspaper *was* the answer.

I wasn't deep in meditation or in the lotus position when my intuition kicked in. Quite unromantically, I was having a cup of coffee and reading the local newspaper when I heard a voice say, 'Call the newspaper. Ask about a sales position.' The voice was relentless and practically nagged me through my doubts until I decided to follow its advice. What did I have to lose?

I dialled the number for the newspaper and this is how the conversation unfolded.

'Good morning, Fairfax Community Newspapers. Can I help you?'

'Yes, may I kindly speak to your sales manager please?'

'Putting you through now sir.'

I had never been called sir before, and boy did it feel powerful!

'Hello, Sylvia speaking. How can I help you?'

'Sylvia, good morning. My name is Jacob Galea. I have just finished reading your local newspaper and feel that I could help make it more exciting to the reader, and build it into a bigger paper. I am not sure if you have anything available at the moment, but maybe we could explore some options ... '

The words just came out of my mouth without any thought.

'Jacob, can you tell me a little bit more about yourself?' asked Sylvia.

Again, my answer was guided by intuition.

'Yes. I am a printer by trade, keen to learn more about sales. I am a disciplined martial arts student, and was hoping for an opportunity to step into a role that could lead me into a dynamic future. I felt guided to contact the sales manager, and so I simply called and asked for you.'

'Well Jacob, that is a very ambitious and brave move, especially as we have no jobs advertised at the moment. But I love your passion. When can we meet?' Sylvia asked.

'I can be there in 30 minutes!'

I put on my suit and drove out onto the highway of the unknown with a big smile on my face.

That afternoon Sylvia offered me a position in telesales. She employed me to build up the auto section of the paper despite there being no job advertised, no vacancy in the sales team, and me having zero experience or training in telesales. I had never even worked in an office. It was way outside my comfort zone, but I did not care one bit. Following my instinct had brought me this far; I wasn't about to turn my back on it now. It also seemed that Sylvia had taken a great leap and followed her instincts to create a position for me. I wasn't going to let either of us down.

I leapt in and took the role by the horns. I was committed with all my heart and soul. I studied sales techniques, asked the managers how I could improve, listened, learnt, and never took my job for granted. I acted as though my role could be uncreated just as quickly as it was created. Now that I had stepped onto the path of greatness where I could live each day with satisfaction there was no turning back. I was so truly grateful for the opportunity and aimed to become the best in that business.

I was a warrior with a mission and within six months I was one of the fastest growing telesales representatives in the team. What's more I was being noticed by the right people. Soon I was being sent to senior management courses and was on my way to business bliss, all because I followed a hunch.

My winning attitude took me further and further up the corporate ladder. Everything was falling into place, like the pieces of a puzzle coming together. I was on the ultimate high – the high of being the creator of your destiny and not the puppet you think you have to be.

However, there is another side to this story …

The job in telesales with Fairfax had so much potential. This was a world where career paths were discussed as part of quarterly performance reviews. I could see this job was the beginning of great things, but there was a catch: it paid less than half of what I had been earning as a printer.

I was willing to follow through on my hunch, but I was not so willing to give up my lifestyle. It is not that I am overly attached to material possessions, but such a drastic cut in income would have meant a considerable upheaval in terms of my living arrangements and a substantial impact on my social life. There were things I could live without, but others I was unwilling to relinquish. So I decided to get a second job to make up the shortfall. The role at Fairfax was by and a large a nine-to-five endeavour leaving me available for night shift.

Intuition had directed me to Fairfax and I felt it had served me well. Fresh on the heels of that magical encounter I threw my fate to the winds once again and called on the same inner intelligence for guidance. I focused on finding the right after-hours position for my journey, stepped up to the board, and … it happened again!

Letting go of the decision, I stilled my mind and began to breathe slowly inwards and outwards. After focusing on my breath for some moments I felt guided to the *Yellow Pages*. I picked up the tome of industry and automatically turned to the local restaurants before calling on my inner warrior to choose the place that would best serve me, while I served.

The advertisement for an Italian pizzeria was practically jumping off the page at me. I dialled their number.

The owner answered, 'La Fontana Pizzeria, Frank speaking.'

I introduced myself and asked if he needed anyone to work evenings. Even after my experience with Sylvia at Fairfax I was astonished by his reply.

'Jacob, you have the most impeccable timing; my pizza maker just left. When can you start?'

That night I started working for Frank. However, my intuition had worked twofold. I had the extra income I was seeking, but my engagement at the pizzeria taught me more than how to make sensational pizza.

Just like pizza, teachers come in all shapes and sizes. To stretch the metaphor, Frank was a life-size, super supreme with an international twist. When I entered the pizzeria, little did I know, I was checking into the school of life. This was a place where the enrolment was exclusive and the wisdom was ancient.

> *Q: What did the Zen monk say*
> *when he entered the pizzeria?*
> *A: Make me one with everything.*

With the right view and right intention the most profound learning may come from the most unorthodox of places. You expect to learn martial arts at a dojo, to become a doctor at medical school, and about cars in a mechanic's workshop. I wanted to learn about the mind, self-mastery and the art of compassion – and I found all of this and more in a humble pizzeria. One of the mysteries in life is that nothing is what it seems.

When you search for things you are most likely looking in the same places that everyone else is. Most often, if you let go of expectations you will find what you are seeking in places you never imagined. By fine-tuning your intentions, focusing on the way you view the world and trusting the answers will come, you make it almost impossible for what you are looking for *not* to find you!

My conscious mind was looking for some extra cash, but my subconscious was fuelled with grander intentions. I looked to my intuition for guidance and it delivered. Had I come to this job with a closed mind, bitter that I needed to give up my free time to slave over a pizza oven, perhaps my experience would have been different. As it was, I quickly recognised and marvelled at the synchronicity that had brought me to exactly where I needed to be. My time at the pizzeria had little to do with making extra cash. It was all about meeting someone who had the ingredients to push me to the next level in the magnificent game that is life.

Frank's teaching began with a smile. That smile had a way of putting people completely at ease and reminding them that life is in the simple things. He showed me, time and time again, that even the worst of days and the darkest of moods can be turned around. The process of smiling can trick the mind and send chemicals through the body, signalling that everything is grand – and since life is only what you perceive it to be, grand it was! I found my childhood smile in that little pizzeria in the suburbs. It was Frank's greatest gift to me.

It is amazing that we allow life to lead us away from happiness. We are almost complicit in its disappearance as we struggle towards our goals and their promise of happiness. We forget that the joy we seek is already before us. In many ways, Frank embodied this most powerful emotion. We sang as we worked, and the pizzas were intoned with the dramatic chorus of *Come Fly with Me*. The warm comfort of garlic, basil and pepperoni could have been a backdrop to a stage in New York City when Frank really got into Sinatra mode. It was absolute escapism. In amongst the cheap red wine, red chequered table cloths and hot mozzarella we were making a difference. Frank greeted each customer like a long-lost friend. If he didn't know their name he knew their order and made it to please. We were cheeky with the clients, and some of them even joined in with the sing-song.

No matter what mood was hanging off someone when they walked in, they soon had a smile on their face. It was just not possible to hold onto a bad notion when confronted by a Cheshire-grinning, Sinatra-chanting, garlic-infused, dough-throwing, tomato-chopping, pizza man named Frank. He was a transformation merchant and I his eager understudy. People looked forward to pizza night with Frank, not for the food, but for the reminder – *life is good*.

In this environment it was easy to lose track of time. I would sometimes get home at 2:00 am and still be at Fairfax raring to go at 9:00 am the next morning. There was real value in how I was spending my time and in my new-found perspective. During this period of my life I didn't have much, but boy was I happy! The idea that material possessions and money in the bank were the only way to contentment and worthiness was blown away.

Have you ever stopped to look at the people in your life and wonder where they came from, why they are there and what you could learn from them? Every single person you encounter is part of your life story. When you have the right view and right intention everyone becomes your teacher. For me, Frank was a master. The wisdom I gleaned from him elevated me to heights I had never dreamed of, by bringing me back to basics.

To be humble, to spend your time and energy wisely, to be mindful and aware of how your attitude determines your outcomes – and to be stoic in your intention to be the very best person you are meant to be in this lifetime – is really all you need. Love and laughter is the glue that holds it all together. Every time someone enters your world, open your mind and heart to them. Feel your way into the scene of your life and ask what role they have been cast as. Ask also what role you will play in their world. It is a two-way scenario. Try to imagine how you connect with their mission as well as how they connect with yours.

Turn to a fresh page in your diary and write down the names of the last five people who have entered your life. What do you feel is the reason they have appeared in your unique story? If you are not sure, next time you meet up, make a point of connecting with them on a deeper level. Have conversations, ask questions and see what comes up. In the process of discovery you might put pieces of the puzzle together that may have gone unnoticed. You will also develop deeper, more meaningful relationships through these encounters. I think of these meetings as ultimate chemistry sessions as this approach to greeting new people into my life has been truly enriching.

Remember, the warrior is a perpetual student. Embrace the people in your life as teachers and listen to their stories. You can learn from both the mistakes and successes of others. The warrior is compassionate and patient. Giving someone a space to be heard, without judgement, can be a great gift indeed.

In loving-kindness meditation, practised in the Buddhist faith, love is extended to one's self and others. This exercise encourages compassion and love for all humanity. Sure, Frank's approach may have been a little different, but the outcome was the same for all who encountered him. Falling in love with life and extending that love to others is one way of knowing you are well onto your path.

So next time you come to a crossroads, stand up, smile, and call up your inner warrior. Be excited to be entering a new stage of your wonderful life. Have no fear! I know the words in this book can take you from being a *worrier* to being a *warrior*. Through this transformation you will become a Super You.

Chapter Five // # Diamonds from the Dark

Most people's inner warrior is buried beneath years of conditioning and mental clutter. Imagine looking for something of great value lost in a filing cabinet with years, maybe decades, of paperwork thrown in with it indiscriminately. It will take time to wade through and clean out the clutter, but you set out with great hope and enthusiasm. You may stumble across what you are looking for in the first few minutes, or it could take months of diligence to sort through and reorder the whole system.

You will be motivated if you think you glimpse your treasure deep in the chaos of receipts and keepsakes. You may dig deep and still not find what you are looking for. You may be distracted by mementos, postcards, invitations, and other odds and ends. You might anguish over the importance of each item and deliberate over what is needed, what is wanted and what is rubbish.

The process may take much longer than you planned as you sort through the disarray and reorganise to make future searches easier. You could stubbornly hang on to awkward, misshapen items that make the search cumbersome, or be distracted by small, shiny objects of no real value or importance. Sometimes you may despair that what you are looking for has been thrown out or lost forever. You may even give up looking. But, before too long, the hope will resurface and pull you back to the hunt.

What you are looking for is too valuable to give up on. You cannot justify leaving this prize uncovered. When you finally put your fingers on it, you recognise it instantly and are overwhelmed by feelings of joy and relief. It was right there all the time.

> *"'I've been through all this
> before," he says to his heart.
> "Yes, you have been through all
> this before," replies his heart.
> "But you have never
> been beyond it."'*
>
> Paulo Coelho

In the mornings, I wore the cape of Fantastic Fairfax – on the phone, in meetings – speed talking my way up the corporate ladder. In the evenings, it was Pizza Passion with Feel-good Fred and his generous sides of love and laughter. I had glimpsed something very important when I followed my intuition to this dual path and I was determined to make the very most of it.

I threw myself equally into both roles and learnt everything I could. I said YES to everything and became completely absorbed in my double life. I was on top of the world and headed somewhere even higher. It never occurred to me that working eighteen hours might have its downside. After about twelve months of candle burning I was sent a huge message.

I woke up one morning unable to move. I was so tired and sick I remained in bed for almost eight days. Living life on double speed caught up with me with a bang. The adrenalin had run out. With grand conviction I had ignored all the warning signs and kept drawing on my inner reserves until the tank was absolutely and utterly empty.

The law of attraction states that like attracts like, and I was a dynamic force of positivity. So when I woke to the glare of morning with pain ebbing through me, aching in places I did not know could ache, I was stunned. I hadn't sent out any negativity inviting illness into my life, so why couldn't I move? Illness had crept up and possessed me overnight. From the tips of my toes to the hairs on my head, it owned every part of me. My vision was blurred, inside and out.

The struggle to fight the reality of influenza was futile. What's more, the inner voice, which had become a constant comfort, had chosen this moment to stop its encouraging chatter and loving guidance. So, as the flu raged through my body, I was stuck in bed for a full week with only my miserable self for company.

The first day was dedicated to shock and denial. Waves of confusion pulsed underneath my physical pain as I tormented over what was happening. I was young, fit, headstrong and on a mission. It just made no sense that I should be struck down when I was flying so high.

By the second day I was just so tired that I simply gave into the pain. I even felt a little guilty for thinking I was better than the flu, but when day three came and the flu was unrelenting I moved straight back into defiance and anger. Surely I had learnt my lesson by now? If it could just be over, I promised, I would never push my body to the limits again ... but that was not enough.

Day four hit me hard and any glimmer of divine purpose had ebbed beyond conviction. The shadows of the sick room were a mirror of my mind. I was thinking and talking like a different person. The mask was off. Fantastic Fairfax and Pizza Passion were revealed to be false crusaders. My shadow-self ridiculed such foolishness.

I was Jacob Galea, plain and simple. Who was I kidding trying to change the plan? I was born and bred for the printing press, and that is just where I would return. If I had just stayed with the program, a puppet to conditioning, I would never have succumbed to a stupid flu.

I questioned my existence, my environment, my entire situation, the choices I had made and my motivations. What was I trying to prove? What was the point of striving and working myself to the point of illness? Giving up seemed the most sensible option, and after six days of battle that is just what I did. That my inner voice had abandoned me through this trial was proof I had been chasing an ego-fuelled dream based on false ideals, unrealistic expectations and motivational misinformation.

However, there was something that could not be shaken. Even when I was overwhelmed by doubt, I did not let go of the idea of a divine universal being. When I gave up on me, this is the energy I surrendered to.

There was no bargaining; my thoughts were sincere and focused. I had given things my best shot, and if I did not have what was needed I would dutifully return to a humble position in the print trade and count my blessings. BUT, should the universe wish to guide me, I would be honoured to serve and devote myself to the betterment of myself and others. It was an incredible relief.

Released from my purpose, free not to climb to the grand heights of a single lofty goal, day seven brought sleep. This was nothing like the feverish bouts of slumber I had endured for the past week. This was deep, soothing sleep that gave rise to a dream like none I had encountered before. This dream accompanied me all day. Later, I wondered if it was too much to take in all at once and, therefore, needed the full day flitting in and out of REM sleep to be able to get the full experience.

The clarity of this dream was startling and I can still recall so much detail. It was very much a lucid dream except I was not an active participant or directing the dream in any way. It felt more like an excursion outside my body rather than a creation of my subconscious because I had drifted into to a world of which I had no recollection or experience. Something acknowledged that I was in Brazil. I was led inside a house with wooden floorboards and with chairs arranged in a circle. I was guided to sit down and was approached by a man dressed in white. His dark hair was just long enough to appear shaggy, but not long enough to be untidy. His deep eyes glimmered behind a modest pair of wire-framed glasses. I did not recognise the man, but I felt at ease as he put his hands on me. He said nothing, but I felt safe to relax and surrender as he carried out some sort of healing ritual. I could feel him physically working on me and the pain start to leave my body.

The next morning I woke up covered in sweat. The sheets were drenched and the fever had broken. My ordeal was over. I was very emotional and tears fell from my eyes in torrents for what felt like hours. Then, almost suddenly, I sat up and got out of my bed pain free! Soon I was having the most amazing shower of my life, washing away every last trace of torment and illness. My spiritual and physical cleansing was complete and I stepped out of the cubicle a new man.

Within a few hours I received a phone call from Frank. He wanted to know if I had ever heard of John of God, a faith healer in Brazil. I was a little bewildered by the question. I had never heard of him, but as Frank spoke I recalled the vivid imagery of my dream.

Two hours later, I received a text message from another friend announcing they were making a journey to Brazil to see John of God. Furthermore, from the barrage of emails that had accumulated during my illness a message from a colleague jumped out at me, lo and behold, about a health retreat in Brazil called John of God.

This was too much. I began to investigate John of God, and the miracle of the internet soon revealed that the man in my dream was indeed this very individual. At this point I was truly reeling. Was it even possible that I could be healed in a dream?

The events of the past week had left me wary of thrilling to any great and meaningful spiritual conclusions. I approached my new reality with patient deliberation, and gently, profound realisation rose in me, not like a firework, but like a new shoot in the spring. Even the darkest night is broken by the golden rays of morning.

An objective observer may scoff that my week in bed was a simple case of man flu. However, the external reality was merely a glimpse of the internal process I had undergone. The physical fever I had endured was symbolic of the inner flame that had torn through my belief system. The filing system of my mind had undergone a metaphoric trial by fire, and ill-formed assumptions, well-marketed mistruths and unproven principles became obsolete. Over the years, I had taken on other people's truths without putting them to the test. In the glare and clarity of first light in the days after my illness I felt freed of the clutter.

There were several lessons that came out of this experience. One was that truth is unshakeable. A universal truth can be applied in all time, space and situations. It can be applied in a corporate boardroom, a game of backyard cricket in the Aussie suburbs and to the twenty-two thousand that die each day due to poverty. So when you read or hear about a truth, challenge it.

Another thing that dawned on me was that we can choose a simple path to wisdom. Many years ago I went to see a renowned motivational speaker. Part of his presentation was to have audience members share extreme success stories. At the end of the talk I wondered at the underlying theme of each example, including his own story. Was spiritual growth accessible to everyone, or was it withheld for those who suffered greatly through near-death experience, abuse or loss?

By choosing such sensational stories the speaker was putting most of his audience out of the reach of spirituality. This is contrasted in other religious disciplines, such as Zen Buddhism, where enlightenment can come in an instant. There is no need to wait for life-threatening illness or crushing emotional trauma to throw your filing system of values, assumptions and beliefs to the flames of the dark night. There are gentle, powerful ways to put truth to the test every day of our lives.

Imagine you are driving down the highway of life. As you speed along bugs of all different sizes bang into the windscreen. When do you clean up your view? Do you wait until the visibility is so poor that it makes driving dangerous? Or do you take the more methodical, steady approach and clear your view as you go? For many of us the view is smeared with years of build-up. We keep adjusting our view, squinting, slowly changing our comfort level, even driving with our heads out the window, until something comes along and we have to stop. The clean-up task can appear so daunting that some people would rather stay where they are, or even drive in reverse, than deal with the rubbish that has built up over the journey.

The good news is you don't have to wait for an accident. You can pull over at any time to scrape the muck off the glass and take a fresh look at the road ahead of you.

Of course if you ignore or deny all the signs and refuse to stop driving, life has a way of putting on the brakes for you ... which leads me to another point. I am not saying that every cloud has a silver lining. I am saying it *can* have a silver lining if you approach it with the right attitude. Now, whatever situation I find myself in, I am constantly asking: 'What can I learn here?'

The law of attraction states that every experience you have encountered in your life was attracted by you. Take a minute to ask yourself whether this statement is true in all cases, across all time, all cultures and all of life. Yes, there are instances when the law is clearly at work. However, there are times when it just doesn't make sense at all.

If you think of a pensioner being robbed at knife point, or a baby being abused, or so many other news items that we encounter every day, the law of attraction holds that the victim is responsible.

This is not exactly the most enlightened point of view, and could have devastating effects on someone who has experienced violent crime by making them accountable for the random action of a third party.

From another angle, a warrior may be drawn to injustice. Not because like attracts like, but because they want to restore balance or create more positive outcomes in the world. We gain another perspective by considering a singer on stage. The most confident, attractive, original and accomplished vocalist will attract attention from theatre companies, recording studios, talent managers and the like. They will also attract jealousy, criticism and, perhaps, even a crazed fan.

However, the benefits of an optimistic approach are hard to ignore. In the bleakest of circumstances a mindset that is calm, collected and optimistic will see opportunities, recognise and accept the hands of friendship and know peace and strength through trusting that where there is a will there is always a way. A positive attitude can manifest in a smile, a can-do attitude, a strong work ethic, artistic passion and much more. Any one of these traits is far more likely to open up doors and create prospects than their negative counterparts. Clearly, a positive attitude is an important part of the success formula.

The illness had refined my thinking and refreshed my viewpoint. The truths that remained had been fired in the kiln of doubt and were now stronger than ever. Best of all the inner voice was back. The warrior remained – louder, clearer, more balanced and stronger than ever. The illness was my wake-up call, and I was a quick enough learner to know that continuing to work eighteen hours a day was not a good call. I stopped, listened, and took the time to learn everything I could from this experience. First and foremost this had been a humbling opportunity to see and understand myself better. As an added bonus the divine being I surrendered to had renewed my purpose through the powerful dream of John of God.

If you drive your car and never service it, pretty soon, you won't have to worry about the state of the windscreen because your car won't be running at all. My vehicle had been well overdue for its one-hundred-thousand-kilometre check. While in for an overhaul I had received a bonus windscreen wash. Hey, there may have been a few cracks in my philosophy once the bug residue was cleared, but nothing that couldn't be fixed.

If you look after your mind and body, your soul can look after itself. The key to self-care is balance. Take time out for fun and love, and, regardless of how hectic your world becomes, plan for regular rest. The greatest problems of the world can be solved in the shower, on a morning walk, or in the first moments after waking from a really good sleep. I cannot stress how important this is for your future wellbeing.

Getting back to practicalities, I was no longer going to treat my body like a machine that never gets serviced. I was now on a new mission. It was time to step up in the corporate world. My goal was to make more money in one job than I had been making in two. That meant saying goodbye to Fairfax and the pizzeria. This was hard. Sylvia had taken a chance on me and Frank had become a mentor. However, my gratitude to them had become a cage of its own. Staying with either position would no longer serve my health or my goals. I had not broken free of the printing press only to replace it with a different environment that did not serve my ambition, purpose and destiny.

Once again I was at a board-breaking moment in my life … and boy was I excited!

Chapter Six **//** # Dynamic Transitions

There is a knack to creating dynamic transitions. We read about happy endings, but in reality, how many of the endings in your life have been happy? Leaving something behind, whether it is a job, a relationship, or an idea about who you are, can be fraught with indecision, insecurity and unresolved emotions. Have a glance over any statistics outlining the life events we find the most stressful and it is all about change. Even positive change can be stressful.

The trick to a dynamic transition is acceptance. Regularly taking the time to map out and review your goals will help you recognise when it is time to make a change. Staying in a career or relationship you have outgrown, or does not correspond to your values and goals, leads to unhappy endings. Someone who stays in a stifling or otherwise unsuitable environment runs the risk of building up feelings of frustration, resentment and anger. A failure to act and make a needed change may lead to toxic situations and a range of unfavourable outcomes. This may manifest as conflict with colleagues, dissatisfaction in other areas or in more extreme cases ill-health, ill-temper and forced change.

Today brings new opportunities; tomorrow brings a new reality.

The warrior seeks to understand their purpose and is able to approach the world with creativity and flexibility. Once you know your goals and have a plan, change becomes an adventure. Your sense of future will encourage you to be proactive and embrace dynamic transitions. It will also embolden you to tap into your courage. Moving towards excellence takes courage. When you stand in courage you are confirming your power, and when you are in your power nothing can move or stop you.

One of the important things I learnt to recognise in karate was the feeling of 'yes'. I approach each situation the same way I approached that board back in the dojo. Before striking, I focus, clear my mind, breathe and wait for the 'yes'. In this 'yes' you have all the courage you need. In the 'yes' you act with clear intention and trust. In the 'yes' you are courageous. Courage is the quiet knowledge that you will succeed. It is simply a matter of connecting to it.

As you move forward, acknowledge the significance of what you are leaving behind. Be grateful for the opportunity you have had to learn and grow. A graceful ending is an opportunity for a wonderful beginning. The next part of your life is completely up to you. As the saying goes, 'God created you; you create the rest.'

Remember, you are always at a crossroads. You can choose to stay idle, or you can choose to move forward with courage. Make your list, know your plan, feel your 'yes' and step into the world with focus. Be mindful that where focus goes, energy flows.

The role with Fairfax had given me the opportunity to build my experience in a corporate environment. My time at the pizzeria had shown me how rewarding and simple it is to see and connect with the people we encounter. For all my gratitude, working both jobs was a scenario that no longer served me. If I had been paying closer attention I would have realised this before my illness. However, I had grown so much through my dark encounter that I had only gratitude for it as well.

Every sunny day is followed by night, and after every period of darkness the sun rises once again. This is the cycle of nature. Even in the most artificial of worlds there is no escaping the natural cycles of life. Life is a cycle of sunny days and dark nights. That is how life works. The warrior learns, grows and stays true to their nature, in the shadows and in the light.

When I tendered my resignation with Fairfax I did so without burning any bridges. I had no job to go to and was taking a big risk. However, it was time to move forward and I knew it would all work out. I was encouraged by the presence of the poised and patient warrior within.

I let go of work altogether. Rather than panic over where my next pay cheque would come from I submerged myself in martial arts training, reading and meditation. The trust I had in my intuition was reinforced through my healing vision and enabled me to relax into my new goal knowing I would be shown the way.

This change was heralded by my illness, but it was my choice. I could have ignored the signal and continued on as before until the change appeared to be out of my control. I chose to acknowledge the sign to put on the brakes and do a life review.

Reflection is an extremely important tool that enables you to dive deep into your thoughts and memories to uncover the clues there to serve you. When you reflect, you connect. Taking as little as seven minutes to reflect each day will help you become the very best version of you. This is a process of stepping into truth, being centred and feeling the 'yes'. Start by reflecting on the day you have just had. Let your mind wander over what happened, who entered your world, what you learnt and how you felt. Ask yourself how this day has made you a better you.

Everything I learnt in my dual life of pizza maker and corporate salesman was now part of my warrior's toolkit. I was grateful for these opportunities, but it was now time to work smarter. Acknowledging you are always at a crossroads, means you always have the power of choice. There is no point in rushing along on a path that is not taking you where you want to be. I checked in with my goals and made my lists. What did I want to change? How did I want to grow? Where did I feel I needed to be? Once I was re-aligned with the inner warrior and my goals it was time to cement my commitment to them with affirmative action. At that moment the best traction was action.

The key to this dynamic transition was trust. I was able to let go of my situation without fear and simply surrender to whatever was meant to be. Without trust it is easy for panic and worry to cloud your choices. By fostering a connection with your inner warrior you build trust in yourself, your intuition and your purpose. Owning the choice to move forwards was mine to make and meant there was no question of falling into a state of worry over how the bills would be paid. I did not enter a self-defeating state of misery or curse the world over my plight. I simply allowed myself to be free, curious and excited about where the next phase of my journey would take me.

Imagine how boring it would be if you knew just how everything was going to happen. It would be like watching a movie and knowing the ending. Embrace surprise and enjoy not knowing, but remain engaged with your destiny. Strengthen your participation by having the right mindset, attitude and spirit.

> *The first sign of success is confidence that one's efforts will bear fruit. The second is being firm in that faith.*

Just five days into unemployment the door to the next chapter opened with a phone call. As open as I had become to the innovative nature of the universe, I remained in awe as I listened to the humble tone of quiet power coming through the receiver. A manager from Fairfax had been raving about my innovative and creative results at a dinner party. I had thus come to the attention of a corporate head hunter in the executive talent search arena. They thought I had potential and was serious about meeting with me to discuss a role that would take my career to the next level. Once again, Mr Unexpected was knocking at my door. 'Always expect the unexpected' is a motto to etch in your thought diary.

When I set off to the meeting I wasn't really clear on what 'the next level' meant. However, I was determined I would not accept anything that did not meet my financial and personal goals. The position on offer exceeded my expectations. Obviously, the agent could see my potential. I was offered the position of sales director for an account worth forty million dollars. The package was worth double of what I had been earning. Cheekily, I asked for even more in the interview and got everything I wanted. It felt right to ask and I went with it. There is a certain magic in connecting to the 'yes' that unlocks the gates to abundance. The position presented me with much more than financial incentive.

With a warrior's mindset I set off into the commercial jungle within the ranks of a company where the corporate ladder soared much higher. I quickly recognised why so many battlefield metaphors exist in business terminology. It was apparent that every move I made was critical. I had been given the opportunity to prove myself and I would need to validate my worth to the company over and over again. This only excited me more as I saw it as a real chance to enhance my tools and knowledge. My constant objective was to remain in the process of becoming the best I could possibly be. This new position gave me every opportunity to do just that.

Every new day leads to new outcomes. You have the power to determine which way the wind will blow in your story. I cannot stress enough just how vital it is to own your thoughts, emotions and choices. When you take responsibility for who you are and who you want to become, you are the master of your universe. At all times, seek to understand your thoughts, your feelings and their influence on your decision-making. The ultimate fusion for your success is to align your thoughts, emotions and the words you speak with your vision for who you are becoming. In this synergy you are assured of being on track to self-mastery. To grow what you want you must know what seeds you are planting. Knowing who you are means monitoring and reflecting on your thoughts, words and feelings.

Bring all aspects of who you are into alignment so you can plant and cultivate the seeds of your desire.

I tackled my new role with every confidence in my ability to perform in the premier league. The title of sales director afforded me freedom. There was no micro-management or corporate negativity hindering my approach. I was free to get in and get on with my role in whatever way I saw fit. The results would speak for themselves. It was like running my own business within a business. The results were solely up to me. I had the joystick. All the company cared about was the results and this suited me perfectly.

This was a very exciting time. I had been graced with the opportunity to tap into my inner power and turn that energy into results. Everything I thought I knew about the ways of the warrior could now be put under pressure and tested with definitive outcomes. I left nothing unchallenged. The mind power, the emotional strategies and all of my warrior tools and tactics were put into action. If they failed in this environment I would quickly be out of a job. However, I had so much faith in warrior that I never considered it a risk. This was a grand chance to experiment with and hone the tools of my inner warrior – and it worked like magic.

Ideas that did not work were quickly left behind. Ideas that got results were sharpened and adjusted for increased impact. Through this period I gained absolute confidence in being Warrior. I was able to identify the warrior's core skill set. In another environment it may have taken decades or even lifetimes to make such progress. However, in this high-end sales environment where results are the only mark of success my team was quick to adapt and take on the warrior's way. Not only was I able to solidify my own experience of warrior, I was able to develop effective methods of invoking this passion in others. Motivating my team and giving them the tools to get the results they were looking for was one of the most rewarding aspects of this role.

These tools are talked about throughout this book. Following the warrior's pathway will ensure you stay on track. Success leaves a trail of clues so you do not have to reinvent the rulebook. You do need to open your mind and heart to all possibilities.

Three years into this role, I woke up knowing it was time to move on. My intuition was communicating loudly with me once again, but this time it was a deeper communication. My inner warrior wanted me to throw away the comfort of a secure salary with a company safety net. It was urging me to fly solo and embark on an adventure that would see me grow in so many other ways. Every warrior knows when it is time to leave the dojo and his master and follow his dharma.

The message from my inner voice was loud and clear: 'Act now!' By this stage I well understood the importance of timing. I had seen the results when I acted on intuition and sometimes more profoundly, the consequences of inaction. It was time to step up to the board and break the next boundary. I was going to start my own company.

It was a big risk. No one in my family had ever started a company, and I had no trust fund to back me up if it all went pear-shaped. I was just an average guy with a dream and a loud inner voice. But you can access your inner voice regardless of upbringing, education, gender, race, or where you live. Absolutely anyone can be a warrior.

I was betting on myself, putting myself out there, and there was no way of knowing what was going to happen. I was making a dynamic transition away from a great salary and a great company. Some people said I was crazy. Little did they know how crazy!

The way of the warrior was calling me, and I was crazily following wherever it would lead. This sent a rush of excitement through my veins. I had a clear vision of what I could build, and this is the key to manifesting anything you desire. See, feel and believe in what you want with every fibre of your soul. Ask yourself what you need to do to make it happen. Trust in your vision, take affirmative action and enjoy the ride.

Besides, what was the worst thing that could happen? If it didn't work out I would just get another job. Even if things did go pear-shaped, I would learn so much through this experience. Giving it a go is the best that you can do. People get locked into the idea that trying can mean failing. However, the only way you can fail is by *not* trying. Not putting yourself forward, not taking that bet on your dreams is failing to live. Don't die with the music still in you!

> *The only way not to make a mistake is to never do anything.*
>
> *The biggest mistake of all is to never do anything.*

Starting a company was yet another opportunity to birth a new me. I loved the feeling of flowing through the process of change. Each time I connected to the warrior within and let myself go with the 'yes' I came across new and exciting ideas and ways of being. I felt that I was in a state of flux – ever-changing, ever-growing, ever-becoming. A week after this dynamic decision to move forward I launched a consulting/coaching business based around the concept of training corporate warriors.

In this new stage, I remained even more committed to the process of becoming the best person I can be – and that is all that matters. Never compare yourself to anyone on this planet. Your underlying plan is to be better today than you were yesterday. Every change I made felt right to me. First and foremost, being a warrior demands that you be the best version of you possible. Strive constantly to be evolving into a super you and you will find this is all that truly matters.

Life is about creating. It is possible to create a new identity and a new reality for yourself. The rush of emotions that has accompanied each of the big changes in my life has been electric. The outward journey is nothing compared to my inner journey.

There is a saying: 'If you do not go within, you go without.' Start your journey by asking yourself how much more you have to offer. Your inner warrior is right there with you ready to guide and support you in creating dynamic transitions and wonderful beginnings. Feel the rush, enjoy the ride and put your unique fingerprint on your creative plan for your abundant future.

Humans are creatures of habit and they resist change. This is why people stay in jobs they outgrew long ago; they are scared to venture into the unknown. But this is what living is all about. Being alive means awakening new experiences; otherwise, you are just existing. We all have dreams and ambitions, but not many people are willing to take a risk and go for it. By discovering your inner warrior you will find the strength and peace you need to live your life with purpose. Have fun, be free, be in control and, most of all, connect with your inner warrior. The warrior within is a wise partner who can lead you into an amazing future.

When you know the power and intelligence that lies within you there is no worry or stress. Challenges become opportunities to change, expand your experience and deepen your knowledge. Awakening the warrior means connecting with the quiet courage and ingenuity that lies within us all. You have found this book for a reason. It is time to create an amazing tomorrow.

Chapter Seven // # Be a Board Breaking Success

The warrior's mindset is a habit. Your mission is to create patterns of thinking and behaviour that serve you. Life is a game of growth. You cannot control everything in life, but you can take charge of your personal growth. Set your goals and let them shape you. When you live with purpose you continue to grow and never get stale or stuck in a rut.

Are there areas in your life that have become stagnant? If you do not feel excited and energised in everything you do, from your relationships to your career, then creating a new approach will create a new you and new results. Changing your relationship or your job without changing your mindset will only land you right back where you are now. Changing your mindset will also change everything around you.

Back in Chapter Three we touched on how our conditioning influences the way we view our place in the world. I have been to seminars and listened to people talk about being deconditioned. That is not how the mind works. Taking all the programs off your computer would not make it more efficient. Likewise, an attempt to free yourself of past conditioning is not going to lead anywhere fast. Creating the warrior's mindset is reconditioning your mind. When you recondition your mind you reshape your emotions and reset your life path. Just as you can replace and upgrade the programming on your computer to make it more efficient, you can choose to upgrade your thinking.

Creating a new habit takes time, patience and passion. At first it can feel like hard work; however, it is just like learning to drive a car. In the beginning there is so much to take in and it can be a little scary. Learning when to clutch, how much petrol you need and simply getting the feel of where your vehicle is on the road can be pretty scary. And then there is the hill start with a possibility of reversing into the car behind.

In no time at all something magic happens. All the information that was daunting and overwhelming becomes automatic. Before you know it you can drive and drink coffee, and talk on the phone (hands free of course!) and negotiate a multi-lane roundabout. You change the gears and work the clutch without even thinking about it. Changing your mindset is much the same. To begin with it will take conscious effort, but before you know it you will be thinking and acting like a warrior with no effort at all.

You can even go at your own pace. I am not asking you to trust me. I am asking you to trust you. I can give you the formula for making dynamic change and share all I know about finding and working with the warrior inside you. I have put everything I am sharing to the test and offer my story as testimony to its effectiveness. I know that it works, but I don't expect you to believe me. However, what have you got to lose by testing this information out for yourself? It won't cost you anything, and you have so much to gain by giving it a go.

Here is a summary of the process we have covered in the previous chapters:

Acknowledge you are at a crossroads. Put on the brakes and have a look at where you are in your life right now. Make your lists – one of the aspects that are moving out of your life and a second of all the wonderful traits of your warrior self. Create and *own* your affirmations. Get to the core of your goals and align your thoughts, emotions and actions with the person you have chosen to become. Identify where you can work more efficiently, both time and energy wise. There is no point rushing off on a new path until you have identified where you want to end up.

Walk your path with dignity, determination and integrity. Know that you define yourself and your influence on the world around you. Everything that has happened to you has already become part of your warrior's toolkit. Nothing has been an accident or a waste of time. You can learn from everything that has brought you to reading this sentence, in this book, at this moment. Observe and remember that you are limitless. The only boundaries and fences around you are the ones you have placed there. You are an infinite being. Your story is still being written so determine to make it a great one. See, feel and know the warrior within you. Meditate and listen to the voice within. What are they saying to you? What can you feel? What do you see?

Always **B**e **C**reating your future by **A**lways **B**eing **C**onscious of how your thoughts are supporting your intentions. Know that you are no longer living with the limitations you knew as a novice. The walls that once limited you no longer exist. In fact they never existed! If you doubt this affirm: 'I am Warrior. I am Limitless.' Cement your commitment to creating your future with positive action.

BE A BOARD BREAKER! Be grateful for the opportunity to make mistakes and face challenges. Let your desire to live, your enthusiasm for creating the best possible version of you and your quiet confidence lead the way. Listen to your intuition.

> *'Listening is a wisdom that*
> *is so easily overlooked.*
> *Listen and your whole life will*
> *become a conversation.'*
>
> Rumi

Learning to trust your intuition is an integral part of this success formula. Trust takes time to build. However, there are so many ways you can build trust in your inner voice. Put it to the test whenever you can. Once you learn to let go and trust in your innate wisdom things will really start to come together for you. The analogy of learning to drive can be applied here. At first it might be hard work even to find your inner voice, and this is where meditation is helpful. As well as turning the volume up on your intuition, quieting the active part of your mind and taking time out for daily reflection will have other benefits.

Just remembering to make a conscious effort to connect and listen to your inner warrior may be hard work at first. But again, in no time at all, the magic will happen. The voice will be there all the time and you will be guided effortlessly by your inherent wisdom.

You will start to be moved by something that is bigger than you. So long as you are clear on your goals for who and where you want to be, after a while, you don't even have to worry about steering.

That is the point I had come to shortly after starting my own business. Things just happened on their own. I did not sit down and map out detailed strategy. Trust, faith, confidence and hope were all the strategy I seemed to need. I surrendered to every hunch I had and made every move from a place of 'yes' as if I had already succeeded. I felt like I had found the instruction booklet for true success. The instructions were very simple:

Be the person you desire to become.
Live and breathe your dream.
Protect it like a mother
protects her baby.
Listen to your intuition.
The rest will take care of itself.

And boy was it taken care of! Everything happened so quickly, I felt like someone had hit the fast forward button. Almost immediately after starting my company I had an abundance of clients. I was featured in every media outlet possible from radio, magazines, newspapers – I even had celebrity clients. If you ask me how all this unfolded I couldn't actually tell you. IT JUST DID. Now I expect nothing less than the best, every step of the way. I own my progress just as I encourage you to own yours.

It continues to unfold around me because I live and breathe everything I want to become. I am the producer and creator of my life. I have found a way of being that delivers the future I desire. The only limits are the ones I have placed on myself.

Yes, I am a work in progress. Whatever the journey ahead holds in store I am ready, poised and excited to meet the challenges and possibilities. Every step I take on this warrior's journey is fuelled by the momentum of every step that has come before it – it all starts with the first step. You took this first step when you awakened the brave new you back in Chapter One. Each step from here on is taking you closer and closer to your desires.

Walking the warrior path means thinking, feeling, learning, living and training like a warrior. Mastering your mind will help you to reach in and listen to the wisdom within. Breaking free of your existing thought patterns can be a mammoth undertaking. Some people spend years talking themselves around in circles in therapy without ever breaking through a single self-limiting idea. In fact, going over and over what went wrong in the past can actually reinforce negative patterns. Connecting to Warrior does not require you to dig deep into past experiences, or understand how your limiting self-beliefs were created. It does require you to commit to raising your awareness of the warrior that exists within you.

Just reading this book shows you are ready to take control of your life. You are set to step up, show up and write an amazing life story. Once the warrior becomes an intrinsic part of your story the script unfolds effortlessly around you. I refer to this process as being in flow. Being in flow is like being in a river that flows towards your dreams. You don't have to swim against the current to get further downstream to where you want to be. When you reach a fork in the river you choose your desired destination and let the river do the work for you. The hard work is getting into the flow and trusting you have thrown yourself into the right stream of consciousness. When you reach this point your future will find you.

Just like giving up smoking, ineffective thinking habits can be hard to kick. Your emotional, behavioural and thought patterns have been established over your entire lifetime. They have been working okay up until now – after all, you are still alive – so it might take a little bit of persuasion to convince your subconscious to take on a new program.

Consider what it generally takes for someone to have a life-changing breakthrough. Losing your job, falling in love, having a near-death experience or a midlife crisis are a few examples. We have talked about risk-taking and stepping out of your comfort zone. The secret is that motivational activities like fire-walking are designed to replicate the brain activity that occurs in a life-changing event. They can push you into a state of flux where it is easier to make genuine change that reaches deep into your subconscious. I am not going to ask you to go parachuting, but if you haven't already done something out of the usual, get out your diary and ink something in right now.

Until the warrior program is hardwired into your subconscious in times of distress, illness or pressure, you may revert to the old ways of thinking. If that happens do not beat yourself up about it. Knowing that this is a normal part of the process means you can recognise it more easily if it happens.

People also find that being in familiar situations with long-term friends and family can bring up old patterns. They expect you to be the same old person you have always been. If you have an older relative who always offers advice or talks down to you then you will understand what I am talking about. It is as if they haven't realised you grew up and can make your own decisions. It is important to be mindful of this. However, there is no need to quit your circle of friends or your family, even if you find some resistance. If they are quick to shoot your dreams down, use the time with them as a challenge to stay strong and true to your new self. By sharing your successes and vision with the people around you, you might even recruit yourself a cheer squad. You may choose to distance yourself from situations where you find extreme opposition; that is okay as well.

|| *Know what you are looking for so you know when you find it!* ||

When you start looking inwards for guidance you may be a little overwhelmed by what you find. Somewhere in the filing cabinets of your subconscious, amongst the whisper of doubt, the cajoling of the trickster and the voice of past dissent, is the beautiful wisdom of your inner warrior. I know that it is there because each and every one of us has this aspect built into our DNA. The warrior archetype was intrinsic to the development of the human race. You and everyone else on this planet has access to courage, discipline, integrity and success. That is just the way it is! The trick is finding it.

It is with great pleasure that I introduce you to your inner warrior. In the chapters that follow I talk about the twelve most important aspects of the warrior within. These descriptions will help you recognise this powerful and wise voice when you hear it.

In your quest for self-knowledge use these chapters like a check list. In what may seem like a contradiction to everything I have said, I don't want you to trust your feelings – at first. This is because your subconscious may be kicking and screaming against the change to your new-found mindset. The feelings you have may be old patterning dressed in warrior's clothing.

It won't be long before you can clearly distinguish between *warrior* and *worrier* for yourself. You will be able to nurture the voice of wisdom and tune out everything else. If you do find the old patterning creeping back you can always come back to the descriptions offered here.

The descriptions are a guide not a dogma. Use my story as an example of how the warrior's way can create dynamic transitions and golden opportunities; I have shared my experience and the following descriptions not so that you can replicate them. Through this book I am offering you a method to etch out your own authentic connection to your inner warrior so that you can write the best-selling story of your life.

Part Two

The Super You!
The Ultimate Guide to
Ultimate Living

//

Chapter Eight **//** Inspiration

I love the word inspiration. The root of 'inspire' is literally 'to breathe into'. The suffix 'tion' means 'state of being'. Hence, inspiration means "to be in a state of breathing in".

Breath is life, so to breathe something in is to be enlivened by it. Being inspired is therefore being truly alive to the possibilities around you. Inspiration is at the very core of this book. My journey into warrior has inspired and enlivened me, and I feel truly alive at the idea of sharing all I have experienced and learnt with as many people as possible. I am inspirited with intention that aligns my emotions, inner thoughts and intuition.

My entourage and mentors have journeyed with me as this manuscript evolved. The entire process has invoked a deep gratitude as I relived my past and came closer to fulfilling my limitless and abundant vision of the future. Inspiration is the WOW factor that links all the aspects of warrior discussed in the next eleven chapters.

Inspiration will move you into action. Through inspiration you will feel connected, whole and purposeful. The question of purpose comes up over and over again in my seminars and coaching sessions. The purpose of one's life is to be the best version of you possible, to stay true to your inner intelligence and to listen to your heart at all times. When you are inspired purpose follows naturally. If you feel you lack purpose I suggest changing perspective. Breathe into life, become enlivened and purpose will find you.

Stepping into warrior is getting into the spirit of things. You are connecting to your spirit as well as the energy of the world around you. This connection excites the field of possibility around you like a build-up of ionised air in an electrical storm and it is only a matter of time before the lightning show.

Plug into positive thinking and the limitless you becomes charged with possibility. A conductive path is formed between you and the heavens so that it is just a matter of waiting for the right moment and, BOOM, inspiration strikes. The point is that inspiration comes naturally to those who breathe into Spirit and charge themselves with positivity. Become inspired and purpose will find you.

Create conductive paths by reaching out to the people you meet and making real connections with them. This is a matter of taking a moment to see who they are outside the task they are performing. Also be aware of the overall atmosphere and feel your way to the possibilities inherent in every situation. This is a process of reaching out or more accurately, breathing in the world around you.

There is no point waiting for inspiration to come along. Every day you spend waiting is just another ordinary day. This is your story, so make it extraordinary. Inspiration cannot sit still. It is a state of purpose, of being moved to action. When you are inspired things will start to happen for you because you will be happening to life. When the lightning bolt of inspiration does hit it is a *lightening* strike. Suddenly things that seemed difficult or out of reach are obviously possible. The disappearance of self-doubt and the fear of change makes achievement almost effortless. In fact, when you are brimming with inspiration it is an effort to avoid opportunities.

Owning your destiny is also a release. Once you have let go of false expectation and your duty to live a life mapped out by others, you will have a lot more energy. Being yourself and living your own life will have its challenges, but when you own your life you also own your challenges and almost revel in overcoming them. You will always have bad days, but you won't be worn down by the effort of living a false life. Being someone you are not is hard work. When you step into your own story you are lightening the load.

Over the next twenty-one thousand words, I want you to breathe in the possibilities that exist all around you. Become enlivened by them and draw closer to your dreams. Anyone can dream, but the real joy in life comes from chasing your dreams. Inspiration is the excited state where your dreams start chasing you back. Be the hero in your story; be enlivened to possibility and you are on the path to becoming the best version of you possible – a super you!

In the first part of this book, I shared my journey with you, so you know this is real. It is absolutely possible to make a dynamic change and start living towards your dreams. Embrace the warrior's journey and allow yourself to be inspired by what you read.

I have broken the warrior's path into twelve aspects. Each step on the journey is linked to every other, but over time I have come to recognise these as individual rocks in the foundation of success. Identifying each of these aspects has allowed me to open others to the warrior's way so they too can find peace, strength and abundance in our stress-fuelled modern world. This is a process of dynamic change that places you as the hero of your story. You can be true to yourself and have success. It is not a fairy tale; it is the warrior's way.

Inspiration is the charge that fuels the process. Who do you want to be in the world? Breathe in peace, strength and abundance and be enlivened by them. You already have everything you need for this journey. It is time to be a greater you!

- Inspiration means 'to breathe into'. Breathe into the possibilities available to you right now.
- Be inspired and you will have purpose.
- Being inspired is creating a conduit for success.
- Inspiration does not wait for life to happen. When you are inspired *you* will happen to life.
- Living your dream is easier than living any other way. It takes effort to be something you are not.
- Breathe into and enliven your dreams. Chase your dreams with inspiration and one day they'll start chasing you back.

Chapter Nine // Vision

In this book, the term 'vision' refers to your capacity to see an ideal you in your ideal future. Rather than seeing with physical eyes, this is a vision that is felt within. You will feel it as excitement or elevation of the soul. Your vision is connected to your dreams and your goals. However, it goes beyond setting down a list of objectives for the future. The warrior's vision is a process of projecting your innermost desires into the future and embarking on the adventure of catching them up.

When I was working at Fairfax and the pizzeria I didn't have a clear vision of my future career. I had plenty of inner vision and energy, just not for the details. My dreams were for success. I wanted to make a difference in this world, help people be the best they could be, create abundance and live a better life. Not being a corporate slave was a point I was absolutely clear on. This sentiment was not directed at the corporate arena as the right role can be very exciting, but I was adamant I would not become a robot, mindlessly slaving away each day for someone else's future. My vision involved me doing something that made me happy. I knew I could create anything because nothing is impossible, and that I could create something that impassioned me. But, I didn't have the *end picture.*

Some say not having the end in mind is an invitation for chaos and disaster. However, I have found the opposite to be true. You don't need to know the end game. In fact, becoming too focused on the details can limit your options.

Working towards a very specific goal can stop you seeing the full spectrum of opportunities open to you – opportunities you may never have imagined when you created your vision board. I have been humbled too many times to think I am the only one with the answers. The universe regularly fills in the blanks in wonderful ways I never would have imagined. This is the fun part to the game. Not knowing what is around the next corner keeps me on my toes and off autopilot. Let's face it: the invisible force that permeates the universe has a broader resource pool than I do. Everyone who walks this planet has access to this intelligence. It is closer to you than you can imagine.

It is essential to have particular goals about who you want to be and where you want to end up. Setting out to become a best-selling author is not as valuable as recognising you have a talent for writing and owning that you love doing it. Knowing what you were born to do is at the foundations of building a super new you. Discovering that you love to sing, build or practise law is like remembering who you are. Stating your vision is as simple as declaring, 'I am a singer', or 'I am a lawyer', or 'I am a business consultant'. So, paint your vision with broad strokes.

Wanting to have financial freedom is a solid goal. You don't need to get caught up in the details. It is important not to confuse your vision with your action plan. If your vision is to be a healer then your plan may include getting into university and finishing a medical or nursing degree. In this scenario it is easy to identify when each stage is complete. If your goal is to have financial freedom your plan may include investing in or starting a business. In this situation it is harder to recognise the time to take the next step. Being clear of your vision also means you don't get caught up and attached to the action plan.

> *Embracing your vision is like finding a rainbow with a pot of gold at both ends. Whichever direction you choose will lead to riches.*

When you are clear of your vision and implement each aspect of the warrior outlined in this book, the end game will reveal itself. As you transform your mindset and step into being the very best person you were born to be, the universe will automatically upgrade your opportunities.

Every master knows the journey chooses them. You can see this basic principle at work every day. Anyone with focus, energy and enthusiasm will be noticed. These people shine like diamonds – they are bright, eye-catching and always in style. People will be drawn to your new energy. It is like a magnetic force. Some people will be ready to jump on board and support your goals. Others will recognise how valuable a person you will be to their business and offer you opportunities where you can really shine.

However you look at it, right now is the best time to be alive and ambitious. The kid who takes this kind of attitude to work at a burger joint won't be making burgers for long. Likewise, an individual who walks the warrior's way will not stay in a limiting environment. Opportunities will knock. And the warrior will be ready to answer.

As you grow, your character is changing. When you think, feel and speak differently your wants, needs and desires will change accordingly. Compare what you thought you wanted at fifteen with what you thought you wanted at twenty. Your values and desires evolve as you evolve. What you think you want today may be completely different to what you want a year from now. Don't hold your vision for the future accountable to what you believe you are capable of today. How you see yourself and your possibilities is changing, even as you read this book.

You are going to come back to your vision many, many times. It will be front and centre in your morning affirmations and your life reviews. Each time you connect with it you come a little closer to making it reality. Repetition will ensure your vision permeates every aspect of who you are. From your conscious thoughts to the depths of your subconscious, your vision will be there.

Construct your vision like expressionist art. Be more concerned with how your vision makes you feel than with the minutiae. There is plenty of room for detail and structure in the planning. When you focus on becoming something – even the greatest something you can imagine right now – you are limiting yourself. Having a vision is like breathing life into who you are. It is unlimited.

Your vision is connected to your passion. Right now you may shake your head or pass off the notion of 'being what you love' as fanciful and impractical, or simply impossible. However, I am not claiming you are going to be woken tomorrow morning by the phone ringing with an invitation from Oprah. A caterpillar doesn't wake up as a butterfly after a ten-minute nap. Stepping into your vision is a beautiful process of transformation, not a cup of instant coffee. It takes a little extra to change from a leaf-munching caterpillar into a graceful, sky-soaring butterfly.

> *'The caterpillar does all the work but the butterfly gets all the publicity.'*
>
> George Carlin

The difference between *ordinary* and *extraordinary* is the *extra*. When I existed in the ordinary world, I did extra reading and study with my mentor. Other extras in my day included affirmation, meditation and information. Slowly but surely, those extras added to my ordinary world to make it extraordinary.

What extras can you fit into your ordinary daily routine to make your world extraordinary? Setting your alarm back fifteen minutes could give you an extra morning breathing exercise, or an extra meditative walk around the block. Trading in thirty minutes of television viewing each evening will give you an extra three-and-a-half hours per week. How you spend that time is up to you. Taking public transport instead of driving will give you extra time to read or listen to motivational audio programs. Having a set grocery order delivered each week could save you time and money. Imagine trading in the time you spend in the supermarket or other tedious activities for time spent studying at a business mentoring group or building your online presence.

Turn to today's date in your diary. Write down everything you could do to add a little extra to your day and step a little closer to your vision. Don't worry about when, where or how you can pay for it—just write it down. I'll give you some examples to get you started, but this is only on the condition that you do NOT limit yourself to the following list.

- Boost your self-esteem! Learn some self-hypnosis techniques, buy an audio program, or see a reputable hypnotist in person.
- Give your wardrobe a dress-for-success finish. A bespoke suit could be in order although having a suit from the local charity store tailored to fit, is easier on the budget.
- Program yourself with positivity. Start every day with meditation and affirmation.
- Exercise your body. A walk around the block, a session at the gym, or a game of squash will help you feel alive.
- Exercise your mind. Study something! Whether it is a short course or a degree, learning something new enriches your enthusiasm and keeps your brain ticking.
- Restock your bookshelf. Have motivational material and information on your area of passion at your fingertips.
- Redecorate. Fill your living space with images that reflect your vision as well as motivational phrases and peaceful scenes.

Consider which of the items on your list would make the biggest difference. Affirmations can be said anytime, anywhere, anyplace. Meditation can be done as you go to sleep, or as you open your eyes in the morning.

So there are some things you can do, starting now. Other things may take a little extra planning. If you want to do some extra study, look at all the pathways available. If you want to work for yourself, get some business cards printed and start making it happen. What you thought was impossible may turn out to be easier than you thought.

Avoid making excuses. I know that where there is a will there is a way. It is all about making a start. Once you step onto the warrior's path of positive change you will be surprised by how quickly those little extras add up and manifest into new opportunities.

Analyse your day. Scrutinise your schedule from sunrise to sunset and look for ways to fit in those extra activities. Look until you find them. Yes, it may feel like a lot extra to start off with; change can be hard work. However, taking a class after work one night a week, or working an extra shift to save some venture capital are just two examples of short-term self-investment with a long-term return. You will draw on the benefits of every extra you invest in yourself for the rest of your life. That is a guarantee.

Again, changing ordinary into extraordinary is about adding the extra. There are enough people in the world doing things in circles and not getting anywhere fast, so it is important to fill your days with activity that connects you to your vision. I want you to add things to your life that inspire you. Study something that excites you. Meet with people with whom you feel a real connection. Choose an exercise you love, in company you enjoy. Yes, you are adding some extra to your life, but it is with things that make you smile, inside and out. By filling your schedule with activities you look forward to, you will have the energy to do more. Enjoying the process is part of the journey.

Every time you add something you love to your life you are walking towards your vision. Remember, you don't need to be too worried by the details of the end picture. It is more about making conscious decisions, taking effective action and knowing that everything you think, feel and do is creating the YOU of your vision. Doing something extra after work because you want to change your job is accelerating you towards change. By investing in change, you let go of any belief that you are 'stuck' in a job, relationship or a situation as well as any idea you have that someone or something else is responsible for you ending up there. So, even the tiniest steps can create big shifts in how you perceive your place in the world.

However, you are also creating a habit of success. If you don't like something you can change it. Finishing a course or picking up a few extra projects for private clients is the beginning of feeling in control. The ordinary droll of living day-to-day will be replaced with a sense of possibility and excitement. And it all starts with the extras.

Have another look at your list. Will doing those things make you feel alive? Will they move you and inspire you to get up in the morning and declare you are on the path to greatness? A few small accomplishments and you can tell yourself with absolute conviction that you are the vision you cast into the future. You just need your skills and circumstances to catch up with the greatness already inside you. By realising this truth, even for a moment, you can enter a place of creation. This is where I activate my imagination and purpose. It is the purest feeling I know.

- Your vision is felt rather than seen. It makes you feel alive.
- Paint your vision with broad strokes. Don't limit yourself with details.

- Knowing who you want to become is more valuable than knowing what you want to achieve.
- Express your vision as 'I am' statements.
- Your vision embraces your passion and purpose.
- When you connect with your vision the universe will connect everything else.
- Ordinary + extra = extraordinary. You will benefit from every extra you invest in yourself for the rest of your life.
- Moving towards your vision is creating a habit of success.
- Activating your vision is connecting to the greatness already inside you.

Chapter Ten **//** Values

Your values determine the character you are and whom you will become. They are the moral pillars on which you are built and represent everything you stand for. You would find them if your character was broken down to its very basic components. They are the qualities that underpin who you are, everything you do and the legacy you will leave behind.

When you value something you hold it dear to your heart and honour it with your last breath. In this chapter, I want you to strive to know your values and to recognise the principles on which your character is built. I value you so much for reading this book and for investing in yourself and your future.

Let's begin by looking at some value statements. None of them are wrong, but they do reflect different ways of seeing and responding to the world on a fundamental level.

- What difference does it make? We all end up in the same place eventually.
- I'm going to spend a long time dead, so I am going to make the most of the short time I am alive.
- Here today, remembered well into tomorrow.
- Who I am makes a difference and I know just what that difference is going to be.
- Life is a game and I am here to win it!

How you value yourself and what you value in others will largely determine the people in your life. Valuing yourself means you will attract people who value themselves. If you value relationships you will develop strong ties and long lasting friendships. If you value intelligence, discernment and courage you will find these qualities among the people in your close circle. The same rule applies to everything you value, whether it is quality time with family, hard work, weekends fishing with mates, or charity work.

It is important not to judge someone's values. Taking time to appreciate that everyone has different values will help you understand what motivates the people around you. For instance, someone who places high value on time spent with friends and family may not be as keen to work sixty hours a week as someone who values material gain and corporate promotion. Subsequently, your values will determine your entourage.

Think about a warrior's entourage. What qualities would they have? The warrior selects these individuals with care. They rely on each other through their successes and it is imperative their values are synchronised. Someone may be courageous, but they might have a value that prevents them from taking advantage or profiteering from certain situations. Although honesty is generally considered a strong quality it may not be accompanied by the value that friends support each other.

People can be different in many ways. So long as they share similar core values a relationship can endure the challenges as well as the good times. Understanding the part your values play in your destiny will help you make some powerful choices about the people with whom you spend time. I am not one for dropping the negative people in life altogether; however, I would encourage you to stand your ground and reduce the time you spend with those who do not support you and your vision. When you value yourself you won't enjoy the company of people who don't do likewise. When you value your time, money and friendships not only will you find people who do the same, but you will encourage the people already in your life to do so as well.

> *'It's not hard to make decisions when you know what your values are.'*
>
> Roy Disney

Do you know what your values are? Open your diary at a fresh page and get ready to discover and declare your values. What do you stand for as a person? Is there a common thread that runs through your relationships, or is there a saying that you live by? Identifying your values will help you navigate your journey towards becoming the best version of you. It will highlight your beliefs and define your ultimate intentions.

Knowing what you stand for will help you choose your battles. You will know when to hold your ground and when to save the fight and your energy for another day. While you should never back down on your core values you reserve the right to review your principles. In this way you can build on or refine your values as you grow through life.

A quick way to discover your values is to have them challenged. Think about the moments in your life where you were cut to the quick over someone's accusations or behaviours. An overt reaction at being falsely accused could reveal a strong value of honesty. If you would rather spend time with your family than stay late at work or go to the bar on the way home, this could indicate strong values surrounding family life.

There are no right or wrong values. When you surround yourself with people who have similar values to you it can accelerate your progress. Aligning yourself with people with different values can cause friction within yourself and your relationships. When others do not respect your values it can keep you at an impasse.

When your entourage shares your passion and values you will all help, support and guide one another forward. In any fitness group there is a core set of people who value fitness and health. Everyone in the group inspires everyone else to eat well and stay fit. It is unlikely this group of people will pressure you to meet them at the local fast food joint. Instead, they may invite you for a bushwalk and a healthy homemade picnic.

Imagine a group of friends in high school. If everyone is keen to do well and go onto university they may have study dates, review each other's assignments or agree to meet in the library after school. In the case where only one person values their education, they would have the constant distraction of party invitations, friends turning up during study time, or being teased for being a goody-two-shoes.

As juvenile as it sounds the same thing could happen for the rest of your life. If you start reading motivational books or attend a night class and your friends ridicule you, really think about what values are at work. If you value yourself enough to invest in creating a better life, then you have to wonder why your friends wouldn't want the same thing for you. It is easy to see that by immersing yourself in an environment and peer group in line with your values it would quicken your progress and see you reach your goals sooner.

It is important to know what your values are before you build an entourage, choose a mentor or go on a date. Remember that you have cast yourself as the hero in your story, so you will require values that will stand up to this role.

Write down who you are and why you do what you do. As you do this, you will understand better where to place your character. Someone who has high ethical values would not want to go into business with the mafia. What's important is to find out what your tribe, values and character will stand for and what they will absolutely not abide by.

Again, it's important to be proud of your values and what they say about you. Being clear on who you are and what you stand for gives you strength of purpose and makes it easier to avoid distraction. Knowing your values keeps you mindful and you are less likely to be led astray. Protecting your values as a mother protects her young is a sure way of staying strong and true to yourself.

This is part of knowing and understanding who you are. You are the captain of your ship, and I urge you to choose your crew wisely. If you don't know what your values are or what your mission is you won't know which crew members have the skills and qualities required.

Most people actually don't know what their values are. They will be upset by someone who is late all the time but never own that they value punctuality. They might be irritated when friends change plans at the last minute without consciously acknowledging they value reliability. If you have strong environmental values you would fare better working with a company that has strict environmental policies in place. There is no joy in turning up to work where your values are challenged. It is so important to understand who you are before you go out into the world.

When you go into the world, be the hero of your story, value yourself and know what you stand for. Take a moment to connect with your heart and accept that you have something special to offer. There is not one other human being on this planet who will experience what you will in your life. Who you are does make a difference, so make it count.

- Your values are the principles on which your character is founded.
- How you value yourself will determine the people in your life.
- Time spent with people who honour your values will accelerate your progress.
- Knowing what you stand for helps you be true to yourself.
- By identifying your values you can avoid losing your identity or being distracted from your path.
- Protecting your values is a sure way of being true to yourself.

Chapter Eleven // Emotions

Entrepreneurs are fascinating people. They can be quirky, reclusive, dynamic, admired, loathed, studious or flamboyant, but there are some characteristics they are likely to share. They are probably competitive, self-possessed and focused, but that is not enough to make a magnate.

There are two very specific ingredients required for entrepreneurial success. The first is knowledge. Somehow or another the entrepreneur will possess all the information they need to make informed decisions and identify opportunities. Secondly, they can see how to jump in and take advantage when the chance presents itself. This trait is intrinsically linked to perception. An entrepreneur not only perceives an opportunity, but also when to strike, who to trust, when to pull back, when to drive hard and when to walk away. Put simply, an entrepreneur knows their business and their instincts.

In the stress-fuelled, fast-paced, internet-savvy world we live in, an entrepreneur must think and make decisions quickly. There is no time for in-depth analysis and labouring over trade reports and financial data. Pondering over facts and figures can mean lost opportunity; so, it is no surprise, entrepreneurs are more intuitive than most.

'Experience taught me a few things. One is to listen to your gut, no matter how good something sounds on paper. The second is that you're generally better off sticking with what you know. And the third is that sometimes your best investments are the ones you don't make.'

Donald Trump

Most people would be surprised, perhaps even shocked, at how many business decisions come down to how someone feels. If I had a dollar for every fortune made on a hunch, well, I'd probably be doing exactly what I am doing right now but in an even nicer suit. There are so many quotes and references linking intuition to success that I won't waste words illustrating the connection here. Rather, we will look at what intuition is and why it works so well for some people.

'The only real valuable thing is intuition.'

Albert Einstein

Einstein was a big proponent of intuition. When you look at Einstein and other specific examples we repeatedly find the connection between knowledge and intuition. If you immerse yourself in mathematics, physics, business or the share market, there will come a time when you intuitively draw on your information stores. This is when trusting your instincts really comes into play. There is a space within you that will connect the dots contained in your conscious and subconscious databanks and give you a result. I am talking about every related little piece of data your mind has ever processed. This includes news items, articles, books, conversations and facial expressions. It is impossible to rationally process all this information, but it is possible to tap into it. This is intuition.

It is important to distinguish psychic impression from the intuition of Einstein and Trump. Being intuitive is about leaping to a conclusion based on information and knowledge you already have that is beyond any rational process. Having this ability immediately puts you ahead of the game because it is not consciously possible to access all the data stored in your mind. A micro facial expression may alert your deep subconscious that someone is withholding information or telling you an outright lie. You don't need to know what it is that tipped the scales in or out of favour, but you do need to trust what you feel. And, this brings us to emotions.

> *'It is through science that we prove, but through intuition that we discover.'*
>
> Henri Poincaré

Your emotions do not lie. They are inner warriors of truth. Your feelings are directly linked to your inner GPS and higher intelligence. Like traffic lights, they can signal an all clear or bring you to an instant halt. Many people have grown and developed in an environment that encouraged them to control or dismiss their feelings. However, emotions have been built into the human operating system for a reason. Ignoring them can have devastating consequences. Acknowledging your feelings can lead you to freedom, success, wealth, health and absolute happiness. However, they are only as reliable as your knowledge; that is, the knowledge of your situation as well as the knowledge of your emotions.

Again, your emotions do not lie. They are the purest form of understanding with which you can connect. How you feel about things is intricately connected to your vision. If you are innately concerned about making changes and unsure about the consequences of breaking old patterns or embracing self-worth, this will be reflected in your feelings. I want you to listen and act on your feelings but first, I want you to understand how they work. What you think and how you have been programmed to feel influences your emotions and how you interpret them. You can probably rattle off numerous occasions when following your feelings led you down the garden path into a side alley and beyond into chaos. Now I am asking you to follow them to success.

Your feelings are akin to an inner guidance system that sways your actions and responses. Have you ever met someone for the first time and instinctively disliked them? If you have ever had a hunch about your friend's new lover or an investment opportunity 'that just couldn't fail' you have probably had your gut feelings confirmed. Most of us have also had the experience of clicking instantly with someone as well. In these situations your soul is communicating with you and guiding your choices. Emotions are energy in motion and, as in these examples, you become aware of that energy in the form of a hunch or gut feeling.

When we talk about the emotions of warrior we are talking about this energy in motion, of recognising a gut feeling and intuitive decision-making. This is not about following a whim or making a decision when you are on an emotional high. This is conscious decision-making that utilises an intuitive process.

There is a myth that intuition is something only a select few are born with and you either have it, or you don't. This is not true. You can switch on and develop your intuition and now is a good time to start.

Intuitive sense is often described as having a gut feeling. This is a clue on how to get started. You are not listening to anxiety that tightens your throat, the love or terror that catches in your chest, or the butterflies of excitement or nervousness at the top of your stomach. You can feel your intuition between your navel and your pelvic bone. Put your hand across that area now and breathe deeply into the pit of your palm. Physically activating this area will help you become more attuned to your intuition.

When your intuitive energy kicks into motion it generally has to filter up through your everyday feelings and assumptions before you start to process them. What starts as a strong, clear signal filters through expectations, learnt responses, doubts, hopes and misinformation. When this happens the message can end up hazy and twisted. Your aim is to listen and act on the signal in its raw form.

Picture your emotional body as a lake. When your intuitive energy comes into motion it is at the deepest part of the lake. The motion swirls up through a rock formation of steadfast beliefs, a boat wreck of repression, sharks of doubt, schools of information fish, eddies of stray feelings and the whale of a mood. By the time it surfaces it is barely recognisable. To connect with your intuition you either need to get right down to the bottom of that lake or dredge the waters until it is clear.

Your role as the captain of your emotional ship is to understand the currents within and how to steer yourself out of the wild seas of life into safe and successful waters. Your emotions are your inner resources' way of communicating to you. What captain would disregard input from loyal, experienced and knowledgeable crew members?

Place your hand flat against the base of your stomach so that your thumb is just under your navel. Close your eyes and breathe in deeply and slowly. Imagine your emotional lake with its ripples, eddies, dolphins and maybe some mermaids. This is your lake, so let it take form in your mind's eye in its own time.

Once you are satisfied with your visualisation dive into the lake until you can touch the bottom. You can breathe under the water so take as long as you like. Explore a little but ultimately, you want to reach the sandy base. When you get there you will find a single rock at the centre. This is your emotional base. When your energy is set in motion this is the rock that moves you.

On this rock, picture a set of traffic lights. Construct them in your mind so when they light up you can clearly see the red, amber or green signal. The lights are now powered by your intuitive energy. As soon as this energy is set in motion the lights will indicate a clear 'yes', 'no' or 'undecided'. From now on, this is the signal you will tune into when you need to make a clear decision.

Swim back to the top of the lake. The sun warms your face as you surface. It is a perfect day. Take a moment to enjoy the beautiful weather before you open your eyes.

Emotional mastery is the most important step in your growth. If you race through a red light in the traffic there will be penalties to face. The same applies if you do not recognise and heed the stop signal from within. From now on you are going to practise accessing and interpreting your gut feelings until you can act on them confidently and swiftly. This is the most powerful way to move forward on something.

Stop. Connect with your body and ask yourself, 'How does this make me feel?' Wait for your body to respond. Picture the traffic lights or feel the truth in your gut. To start with, use it for anything you can think of. Begin with simple decisions and build to things that will have a bigger impact. Push yourself forward with this exercise so you become increasingly confident about your instincts until you know you can count on them. Make decisions within. Never act unless you feel the green light of an absolute YES.

If you want guidance or answers, have a conversation with your master emotions. Your master emotions are your heart and traffic light system combined. Visualise a power cord from your heart to your emotional rock and plug it in. Most people's inner warrior is buried beneath years of conditioning and clutter. Connect to your true emotions and you will uncover the warrior sleeping within.

Once you switch on your master emotions you will realise how unnecessary all the clutter is. Most of it will simply disappear. As you read this book and put the exercises into action you will be changing the form of your belief system and starting to clear away the wreckage.

The warrior aims for emotional clarity. Emotional intelligence is knowing what you are feeling and why you are feeling it. You can listen to your emotions without being controlled by them. As a warrior you can even change how you feel about something. If you have negative feelings about a job interview you can explore those feelings and rethink your responses. Before any important meeting, connect to your emotional base and breathe deeply through the clutter of emotional melee until you feel an unwavering yes rise within you. From this place of yes, everything is possible. When you feel this yes, the universe says yes to you.

- Entrepreneurs know their business and their instincts.
- Your instincts draw from all knowledge and experience in your conscious and subconscious databanks.
- Your feelings do not lie. You do need to know how to read them.
- Emotions are energy in motion.
- Being aware of your inner traffic lights will help you make stronger, faster and clearer decisions.
- Consciously make intuitive decisions through emotional mastery.
- Focus on your master emotions and seek the emotional clarity of a warrior.
- Feel the yes in your inner world and you will find the yes in your outside world.

Chapter Twelve **// Intention**

Throughout my journey, all of my mentors and spiritual teachers have asked about my intentions. Achieving your goals means changing how you see the world, how you approach each moment, perhaps even who you are. If you have no intention of transforming your life and no desire to step outside the comfort of your current routine, it is unlikely you'd ever achieve your goals and desires. Your intentions pave the road you walk on. Set your intentions high and your path will be elevated.

An intention is a lot more than a statement about what you propose to do at some point in the future. It is a force that can move the universe. Your intentions must be felt deep within you. Give them the full attention of your emotional self. That is, get your emotions on board so they fuel your intentions and propel you forward with focus and confidence. Be excited about what you are going to do.

At first, stating your intentions may make you feel stupid, embarrassed or egotistical. By all means, take some time out to explore those feelings, but don't change your intentions. Keep making your statement. Declare it out loud to yourself until you feel the excitement brimming inside. Pronounce your intention in the morning, in the evening and at every opportunity in between. Share it with strangers as well as friends until it feels like the most natural thing you could possibly do. Say it until the anticipation exhilarates you.

Re-read this until you have it embedded in your subconscious. You need to feel your intention. It has to move your soul and excite you to action. Your emotions will drive you forward and make your intention a reality.

Intentions can act as a filter. Someone who picks up this book looking for tips on how to make a quick fortune will filter the information in a different way to others who are looking for inner peace, wanting to build their confidence, or striving to become the best salesperson in their field. The information that strikes a chord with your intention will stand out from the text and stick in your memory.

This information filtering and tagging process is happening all the time. Whether you are in the supermarket, networking, or in a business meeting your mind is alert to data that supports your intention. If you want to buy a boat, anything to do with boats will catch your attention as you have turned on your boat filter. If you want to fast-track your investment strategy your wealth filter will be switched on. If you want to enter a new career path, bells will ring when you are introduced to someone who works in your field of interest.

You might have encountered all this information before, without taking much notice. Once the information falls within your field of intention it peaks on the radar. When you set clear intentions you will find information and opportunities appearing before you. This is the magical formula of manifestation. You probably noticed the same phenomenon occur the last time you bought a new car. Suddenly there are cars of the same make, model and colour everywhere. They were always there, but you never noticed them. Now you can't go anywhere without seeing one. This is why it is important to make your intentions very clear to your conscious and subconscious self. By doing so you elevate your pathway of possibility to the height of your intention.

Intentions are like steps in the game plan to achieve your vision. For example, if your vision is to be a writer you may intend to do a writing course, join a writers' group and submit a manuscript before the end of the year. You may start the writing course with the intention of blitzing it and getting noticed by the lecturer. You may also intend to stir up some political drama, or bring attention to a social problem or health issue through your work.

Once you really lay down your intentions anything you come across that can help you achieve your goals will grab your attention. If you are in a room full of people you may overhear a conversation about a writers' workshop or be introduced to an author who can give you some tips. The same will be true whether you intend to start an investment portfolio or sail around the world. Your ears will be tuned to hear things they have never heard before. Likewise, your eyes, emotions and intuition will be on alert for all things connected to your intention.

|| *'There is always a gap between intention and action.'* ||

Paulo Coelho

If someone asked about your intentions could you give them a clear answer? How would your answer make you feel? What actions will you take to fulfil them? In order to identify your intentions and the reasons behind them, simply write one down on a fresh page in your diary. Begin with 'I intend to' and fill in the rest of the sentence.

Here are a few examples:

- I intend to earn an extra fifty thousand dollars next year.
- I intend to audition for a theatre company.
- I intend to launch a new website.
- I intend to buy an investment property.
- I intend to retire early and move to the seaside.
- I intend to make friends with the same interests as me.

Once you have written down an intention take a few minutes to consider why you want this particular thing. Of all the options in this world, why have you chosen this one? It is important to understand the 'why' behind your intentions.

Let's take a look at the first example. Let's say Alice intends to earn an extra fifty thousand dollars next year. This is a fine goal to have, but why is it important to Alice? The answer can be very revealing.

Answer one: The extra fifty thousand dollars will enable me to save enough money for a deposit on an investment property.

Answer two: I've been working for the firm long enough and if they don't give me a promotion and the pay rise I deserve, I'll quit.

Answer three: I want to earn more money than my hoity-toity sister.

Answer four: An extra fifty thousand dollars per year will pay to
    build a granny flat. We can then get a live-in nanny which will
    increase the quality of life for me and my kids. We'll have less
    stress in the mornings and so much more quality time together.

It is important to have a strong reason why. This will keep you on
track and focused. If you don't understand why you want something,
quite often, it won't manifest. If you want to be a millionaire, but
you haven't really thought about why, then you haven't given your
goal any substance or urgency. The why is the motivation behind
your intention. Without it, your purpose has no heartbeat.

Your intentions lay down the pathway towards your vision. They
identify the bricks and stepping stones for each step you take. The
more alive and free your intentions make you feel the more readily
you will reach them.

If you are not comfortable telling people about your intentions,
this is another area to explore. If you want to become an astronaut
look people in the eye and tell them with confidence that this is
what you intend. Blow them away with the power of your conviction.
Investigate your pathway, know the steps you need to take and tell
people your plan to start a mathematics and science degree. Tell
them how this will lead to opportunities in the space program.

Every time you repeat your intentions out loud you energise
them. When you share your dreams with others most people will
champion you. The person who tries to shoot you down is giving
you an opportunity to address any reservations you have. When you
respond to outside criticism, or answer a qualm, it is a chance to
affirm your goals and make your intentions more clear. The funny

thing is, the more confident you are the less you will encounter objections or doubt from others.

Looking at the reasons behind your intentions should make you feel stronger and more motivated to achieve them. If you are wavering in any way, give them the traffic light test. If your reasons makes you feel amber or red investigate your intentions a little further. Ask yourself why you feel that way. Keep asking until you identify the basis for your hesitation.

Being scared about making a big change or of failing is no reason to change your intentions. However, once things start to surface you may discover that your intentions are not connected to your heart space. Perhaps it is a lingering desire to please a parent, or to show someone you are worth more than them. Will achieving your intention bring you real joy, or create a bigger emotional need than you have now?

Undertake this review process honestly and brutally before you commit to an intention. It is best to know whether your desire is an extension of who you truly are, an elaborate tactic to avoid who you are, or an attempt to be the person you think you are supposed to be. It is hard to stick with things when the motivation isn't founded in a space that makes your heart sing. Of course, your heart can sing to the tune of revenge or 'I told you so', but the tune will be shorter-lived than the anthem of 'I love who I am and what I do'.

'I believe the choice to be excellent begins with aligning your thoughts and words with the intention to require more from yourself.'

Oprah Winfrey

Your heart and emotions give life to your intention. Once you feel that life inside you it is your job to keep nurturing your intention until you are well on your way to achieving it. You have to absolutely nurture its growth and development. By exploring the reasons behind your intentions you can ensure it is planted in the right soil. Once the seed is planted you can water it with positive emotions and feed it with repeated affirmation and determination. Take definite action towards your goals without strangling them to death. Remember to enjoy the journey and allow yourself time to relax and enjoy the people and world around you. Remember: don't let your intentions put you in tension.

Without setting strong intentions you run the risk of drifting through life with no real purpose. Yes, it can be interesting to go from one thing to another just seeing where life takes you, but sooner or later most people start to want the satisfaction that going with the flow won't ever provide. If you are not committed to something in life people are unlikely to offer you a job or an opportunity. If you are unsure of your intentions others will be as well. Without purpose you may come across as unreliable, detached or without focus. These are not qualities that go hand-in-hand with success.

You can intend to be anything at all, but if you don't take positive action towards your goals they won't be taking steps towards you. Intention without action is not purposeful. Declaring you have a goal without doing anything about is akin to wanting roast beef for dinner without turning on the oven. As soon as you start to make progress for yourself you cement your commitment to success.

You see, your actions and your progress will inspire you onwards. Other people will see this as well and give you encouragement and assistance. Everyone loves a hero, and turning your life into a success story is nothing short of heroic. When you live out your story of success you leave a legacy to inspire future warriors.

The aspects of intention can be broken into four key areas. Your intentions should be connected to your soul as this houses your life script. Your intentions should move you emotionally. You should understand the motivation behind your intentions and then be inspired to take positive action towards them. With this formula you engage your spirit, heart, mind and body, and that means you are committing to your goal with every aspect of your being. This really puts some power behind your resolve. I believe this is why the warrior's way gets such great results, over and over again.

- Your future is mapped out as your subconscious tags and filters information aligned with your intentions.
- When you set clear intentions you will find information and opportunities appearing before you. Your intentions bring you closer to your vision.
- The reasons behind your intentions are their foundations. These reasons are your motivators.
- It is wise to explore the whys before committing to your intentions.
- Your heart and emotions give life to your intentions.
- The warrior connects his/her intentions to their mind, body, heart and soul.

Chapter Thirteen **// Be Limitless**

If you want to be happy, be happy. If you want to be abundant, be abundant. If you want to be free to live to your full potential as the very best version of you possible, be limitless. The words we use to describe this state of freedom reveal how hard it is to grasp. We define it by what it is not: not having limits, not knowing boundaries, not living to the expectations of others, and not being caged by conditioning. I have strived to find a word that declares limitlessness for what it *is* rather than what it is not.

To find this word I pondered on who I am without limits, boundaries, conditions, false expectations and caged desires. And the answer was obvious. I am ME. To be limitless is to be authentic.

From this moment on let go of your quest for perfection and start striving for authenticity. It is on this path you will know and be the limitless warrior.

|| *'The privilege of a lifetime is to become who you really are.'* ||

C G Jung

We are conditioned from a young age to be average. Where you are today is not where you have to be tomorrow. You, as the limitless warrior, know there are endless choices radiating from the crossroads every moment of your life. Right now you can make a decision that will change your destiny. Countless options have always been open to you. However, you have only been able to see the ones that fit with your perception of who you are.

Have you ever seen a circus elephant chained to a peg in the ground? The elephant could easily pull the peg out and run free. However, the elephant has been conditioned from an early age to know that attempting to be free of that chain is futile. In time, the elephant doesn't even have the urge to try to pull on the restraint.

Just as we express being limitless by what it is not we tend to assert our desire for freedom by what we no longer want in our lives. The limits we place on ourselves can be so ingrained in who we have become that they remain hidden and difficult to identify. Just like the elephant, we simply accept the restraint as reality and give up trying to fight it. After a while, you forget what it is you have lost. In some cases, we never know any other way, and you can't miss what you never had.

This is why being authentic can be a very daunting task. However, it is worth the effort of breaking free and, like the elephant's peg, it will be much easier than you think. Once you step into limitlessness you will revel in your freedom; but, like a bird who has been hand-raised, it might take some practice before you feel confident enough to truly fly free. In time, you will come to trust that authenticity is a strong and resilient foundation that will not be shaken by the stress and pressures of the modern world. Start simply by stretching your wings as often as you can.

Write down how you are limiting yourself right now. If you are not in the career of your choice, or taking steps towards being in that career, you are not living authentically. The same applies for the other areas in your life. What are your reasons for not being true to who you are? Make a list of everything you think is keeping you in your current situation.

Next to these limitations write out your position statement. This is a statement of where you are right now: where you live, where you work, your occupation, your income … everything about your current position in life.

Once you have your current reality down in writing, I'd like you to think about expansion. Your current life position exists within an infinite realm. You exist in a universe that is limitless and still expanding. Wherever you are right now – in a room, in a house, in a suburb, in a state, in a country, on a planet, in a galaxy – you are in an expanding and limitless universe. You and your life position becomes static only when you give it labels.

When you define who you are with limiting labels you step out of the natural pattern of the universe and enter a constructed dimension where things do not grow or change. If you are conditioned to think, feel and see yourself as incapable, lazy or middle-of-the-road, then these labels will keep you jailed in a state that is not authentic. This state looks and feels real. It feeds back to you whatever you are conditioned to see. Your perception is coloured by your limiting beliefs.

Hans Christian Andersen's tale, *The Snow Queen,* teaches us how self-defeating our perceptions can be. When the young hero gets a piece of magic mirror in his eye it distorts the way he sees the world. The tiny piece of glass is no bigger than a grain of sand, but it gets into his heart and turns it cold so he only sees the bad and ugly in all things. He no longer cares about the people in his life, and when he is offered kindness he interprets it as manipulation. The boy is taken by the Snow Queen who directs his negative perception at the outside world to keep him imprisoned. Of course, this tale has a happy ending. The love and innocence of his devoted young friend melts the ice in his heart. He is able to see the world in balance once again and is freed.

Change your perspective and the world will reveal itself to be a different place. Get rid of those limiting labels. The warrior is unlimited. The warrior walks a path without ending, constantly redefining his/her place in the world. By the very nature of their authenticity the warrior is always growing, learning and expanding. Whether your objective is to get a job and pay some bills, spend more quality time with your loved ones, buy a new home, or step into your ultimate dream career, when you connect to the warrior within there are no boundaries. Everything becomes perfect and whole.

> *Through imagination your potential is limitless. Break through the boundaries of perception and discover the infinite possibilities open to you right now.*

I can share three secrets on how to be limitless. First of all, live in a state of becoming. Do not label who you are now. Think of yourself as the person you are going to be. Act as that person, dream as that person, give off the aura of that person. Be in the present as you strive to be in the future. Your current persona will attract a fresh reality like a magnet. Your thoughts are the currency that buys your future.

Another key to unlocking your limitless potential is owning your beliefs. Never underestimate the power of belief. What you believe is an intrinsic part of your mythos. It determines how you write the story of your life. These beliefs have been built over your lifetime and are rarely noticed until they are challenged. Connecting with warrior will challenge who you think you are. If you believe you cannot, should not, will not succeed – these beliefs will be shaken. As warrior you have the power to choose what you believe. You are the author of your story. Step into the part of the hero.

You may have done this exercise or a version of it before. Today, I want you to do it with authenticity, passion and belief. You will need pens or pencils and some blank pieces of paper.

Imagine what your life looks like without boundaries. Write about or draw your perfect life. You can create any reality at all. Take your time, be bold, be daring and be truthful.

This is a glimpse of the limitless possibilities available to you. Compare this to your current life position. What steps will you need to take to change it to this possible reality? Do not be daunted by the size of the journey.

The third secret to becoming you, unlimited, is purpose. When you live with purpose, on purpose, you are constantly reducing the gap between your current position and your new borderless reality.

Through authenticity you will find clarity and strength of purpose. Affirmative action is a natural by-product of a limitless you.

When you step into limitlessness you will follow through on your goals. I see so many people give up on their dreams when doubt creeps in or things get too hard. This is because they missed some steps in their success plan. Being limitless is a mindset that is switched on when you activate the warrior within. Once the transformation is made there is no chance of turning back. Once you see it, you cannot 'un-know' that you are limitless. The old way can no longer exist for you.

The path of warrior is easy to walk. It is just a matter of putting one foot ahead of the other. You can set your own pace, make the occasional diversion or fast-track your adventures ... but you won't quit. That is the only thing that remains impossible.

- Being limitless is being authentic.
- You can replace your struggle for perfection with the pursuit of authenticity.
- You are always at a crossroads of infinite possibility.
- There are no limits except the ones you have learnt to place on yourself.
- You can make a decision that will change your destiny, right now.
- A change of perception will open up a whole new world.
- Your thoughts are the currency that buy your future.
- You are the author of your own story. Write yourself the part of the hero.
- Affirmative action lessens the gap between your current life position and becoming 'you unlimited'.

Chapter Fourteen **//** # Inner Dialogue

If you were stranded alone on a desert island would you be in good company? In isolation, the importance of your inner dialogue would be exponentially magnified. Your very survival could count on it. Actually, it would count on it. This extreme hypothetical situation quickly reveals humanity's biggest fears: failure, rejection, madness, the unknown and death. Note that death is *not* at the top of this list.

For some people dying at sea is preferable to washing up on a desert island. On an island there is no one to blame or rely on. There is no one to encourage or ridicule you. There is no one to lead and no one to follow. There is no one to tell you your ideas are crazy and no one to tell you they are brilliant. That is, no one besides you. You are responsible for your destiny. How do you think you would go?

Take your time with this chapter and really consider what goes on inside your head and soul. I want to show you there is more to self-talk than meets the 'I'. The warrior's way is not about self-help;

it is about self-mastery. So I urge you to let go of what you think you know about positive thinking and be open to learning this approach anew. The warrior's approach is about aligning your head and your heart. This navigation system is so intelligent and reliable that when you switch it on you will be guided to a life you only dream of.

Self-talk is a little like gravity. It is there all the time weighing things down. It is such a normal part of everyday life it can easily remain an invisible force unless someone comes along and points it out. Once discovered, the implications are so obvious you wonder how it went unnoticed for so long. Likewise, when you are aware of your self-talk it is impossible not to see the impact your inner voice is having on the way you experience every moment of your life. Of course, just like inner dialogue, gravity is a universal force of attraction. It is the Holy Grail of human success and your mission is to find it, connect with it and nurture it.

According to Newton's law of universal gravity, all objects are attracted to each other with a force of gravitational attraction. The force of the attraction is determined by the mass of the objects and the distance between their centres. When we apply the same universal principle to our inner dialogue we see that the form of our thoughts and where they are centred determines the force of attraction.

The mass or form of your thoughts determines the strength of the pull. The bigger the object the stronger the attraction. If you treat your goals like a passing fancy or see them as part of a distant, impossible future then the thinking that surrounds them will be lightweight. When you commit to a goal and nurture it over time you give it more space in your mind. The more space the thoughts take up the stronger their force of attraction.

It is essential for self-belief to be at the centre of your thought system. When you doubt your potential your inner dialogue will not be centred on your goals. When you are off centre it is all too easy to become lost or stuck in a rut.

Life can be filled with distraction instead of attraction. This distraction can lead you down a wrong path; it can take you so far away from truth and your soul's purpose that it may take years to get back on track. Of course, however far you stray from your desired life it is always in reach. It is never impossible nor pointless to step into change and begin the journey to limitlessness. In some cases, straying off course can make it easier to stay true to yourself in the future.

Your inner dialogue is not just about what you say to yourself. It is not just about how you feel. Your inner dialogue is everything that happens within you.

Getting back to our desert island: how is your relationship with your inner warrior? Are you in good company when you are on your own? What do you think and say about yourself all day long?

Simulate the island experience by setting aside an hour, a whole day or longer, to be completely on your own with your thoughts. There is to be no radio, telephone, television, books or other outside distractions. The only person you can talk to is yourself. If you don't find your conversations supportive, loving and constructive you could do with a mental intervention of the warrior kind. I call this having a chemistry session with yourself!

To successfully implement a mental intervention it is important to note the different ways we talk to ourselves. First up, there is motivational talk. This is the type of inner dialogue most commonly linked to positive thinking. There is also instructional or cognitive dialogue, as well as reflective and incidental self-talk. In the warrior's mental intervention package positive thinking is applied to each of these areas.

Hold supportive, loving and constructive thoughts all day long, not just in the morning or in your evening meditation. Don't let positivity get away from you. Many minds are like drifters with no focus or direction. Say to yourself daily, 'I am constantly moving forward and transforming into greatness and inner power.' Even when you don't believe the great things you are telling yourself, keep on saying them. I am not telling you to push aside or ignore sadness or anger; repression is never a good start to an honest and energetic experience of life. Emotions in themselves are not negative, they are indicators that something is not quite right. Exploring your emotions and seeking to identify the true source of your feelings is part of the journey of self-discovery. However, it is important to keep on top of any negativity directed at yourself.

Criticism, doubt, abuse and a preoccupation with comparing yourself to others are like weeds in your garden. If you do not pull them out by the roots they will take over and stop the seeds of success and happiness from blossoming and bearing fruit.

At the moment, your mind may be overrun and tangled with undesirable thought patterns. This is true for many people as so much of what we think and do is habitual. In this case, negative self-talk can be the automatic response to any opportunity or change that life brings us. Roll up your sleeves and get to work in your mind garden. Once the big, initial clean-up is done, you need to do regular maintenance to ensure the weeds of negativity don't start creeping in again.

The key here is being aware of what is happening within. Your external world is merely a reflection of your internal world. To custom-build your outside reality it is imperative you address the fine details of your inner talk. If this was easy, everyone would be healthy, wealthy and happy.

Paying constant attention to your thoughts, words and feelings is hard work. Changing your mind takes persistence and passion. If at first it feels like you are pushing a boulder up a hill it means you are doing it right. And WOW, things get much easier on the other side of the bump!

Once you discover and begin caring for your inner garden it will blossom with inspiration, creativity and imagination. From this garden you can create a pathway to abundance and a world of limitless possibility. This garden is also your sanctuary. In the hustle and bustle of this stress-fuelled world you will always have somewhere safe to retreat. Your mind garden will provide nourishment and peace any time you need it.

Your self-esteem can be the toughest hurdle in programming your self-talk to its optimum setting. Once you get your subconscious to realise your awesomeness everything else falls into place much easier. Some people look so defeated when I talk about self-esteem. Years of therapy may improve a person's understanding of who and why they are, but do very little to improve their self-worth. The warrior in you knows your value. When you activate the warrior within you must be ready to let go of any self-doubt. It is not serving you, you don't need it and, quite frankly, you outgrew it long ago. Self-doubt is not for grown-ups. So flick the switch.

No one is born with low self-esteem. If at some point in your life the esteem setting in your subconscious was set to low, I want you to change it. Visualise the dial and turn it to high. Actually, turn it to very high. Hey, just switch it to awesome and be done with it! Anytime doubt creeps in check up on the setting and switch it back to where it belongs. Job done!

But wait, there's more …

At the same time as you motivate, direct and dream yourself into a vibrant and centred force of positivity, I want you to be aware of the words you use. In particular, be on the lookout for repeated and high-use vocabulary. The words and phrasing you use are vibrational and are part of the currency buying your reality. Remember, your subconscious doesn't know the difference between reality and fantasy. It can't tell what is intentional affirmation and all that other stuff it isn't supposed to be taking notice of. So mind your language. To your subconscious, vulgar colloquialism carries the same weight as a well-crafted mantra. If you are a frequent user of expletives I urge you to think about what your subconscious is be full of.

Our language skills are developed as we interact with others. Sometimes we pick up sayings and routine responses without ever thinking about what the words actually mean. So I want you to think about what you are saying. I also encourage you to mix things up a little. Try out some new and experimental responses to the standard questions we encounter in everyday life. For example, when someone greets you and asks how you are don't answer with mediocrity. Respond with something magnificent, something electric.

Your words can be powerful so be sure to use them wisely. If your words are flat you will get a dead flat response from the world. Likewise, when your words are charged with positive intention the world will respond in kind.

> *"Then you should say what you*
> *mean," the March Hare went on.*
> *"I do," Alice hastily replied; "at*
> *least – at least I mean*
> *what I say – that's the same thing,*
> *you know."*
> *"Not the same thing a bit!" said the*
> *Hatter.*
> *"You might just as well say that*
> *'I see what I eat' is the same*
> *thing as 'I eat what I see!"*

Lewis Carroll

You can spend years of therapy trying to solve the mystery of your subconscious mind. It can be a daunting place to venture. However, the beliefs you hold in your subconscious have a tremendous impact on your life, so venture there you must! For all its power and mystery you now know its weakness: it doesn't know what is real and what is imagined. Now that you realise what a fantastical place the subconscious is you can actively fill it with a new story. When you close your eyes and visualise success the labyrinth of your mind absorbs the experience as if it is real.

Create a mental movie. The creation of your mental movie begins with a limitless script. It is essential you know exactly where your movie is heading.

For example:

I have a *New York Times* best-selling book that helps people achieve their greatness. This book is helping sick people become better. It is helping business owners become greater. I have authored a book that is at the pinnacle of self-mastery for the twenty-first century.

The scene begins at a book signing in New York. It is time to go as I am booked on a national talk show. As I make my way to the limousine someone approaches me with a smile of gratitude and tells me how the book has inspired them to change their life in ways they could never have imagined.

Once you have your amazing script and cast yourself in the role of the hero, it is time to sit back and watch the adventure of your lifetime. Sit in an upright position, close your eyes and pretend you are in a cinema with a screen in front of you. You are the producer, the actor and the audience.

Now it is a matter of producing the scenes so they play out exactly the way you want your life to unfold. The sharper you make the detail in your mental movie the bigger and more real it will be to your subconscious. Bring it to life with full colour, surround sound and honest emotion. This is your very own Hollywood blockbuster—own it! Give the performance of your life! Enliven yourself for success in the real world; be confident and innovative.

As you watch your scene unfold, see the colours, hear the words and connect with the scenery. Above all, let yourself connect to the story and feel the emotion. Through your mental movie you are actively participating in the creation of the most rewarding role of your life. This is you cast as the very best version of you possible.

Let this movie make your heart sing. Be electrified within when you watch it.

Play this mental movie repeatedly. Each time you hit play bring more detail and emotion to your role. With each repetition the message of success is etched a little deeper in your mind. Each time you live out your role you connect to the confident, creative, most auspicious version of you. This process lessens the divide between the current you and the greatest you.

When you open your eyes take a moment to engage with the feelings that have arisen during the screening. These feelings may include courage, enthusiasm, relief, and the need to shout for joy, or a deep, quiet confidence that everything is falling into place. Carry those feelings with you into your everyday life. Carry the qualities of the hero of your film as well. Let yourself believe in your greatness. Act as if the scene in your movie is a real part of your future. Know that it is just a matter of time before it happens.

Now you have your script and your mental movie. You believe inside that this is who you are and what you will achieve. Now you have to speak out loud and act as if you are that person. After years of engaging in this process I have absolute trust in it. I write the scripts for my mind movies with increasing flair and assurance. After each visualisation I am confident it is just a matter of time before the reality of my inner hero unfolds. I am not attached to the details of the scene or the script. The setting may be different, but the confidence, charm and success of the hero stay with me.

|| *Speak not of who you are but in confidence of who you will become.* ||

There is no trace of doubt in any cell within me. I will not be surprised when opportunity presents itself. I will be prepared, grateful and awestruck at the way invisible forces move the pieces into play. However, I am not surprised and nor will you be.

You created it! You planted the seeds and nurtured the new you until the outer reality caughtt up with your inner reality. This is manifestation. Believe it, feel it, speak it, live it, BE IT!

- The warrior strives for self-mastery.
- Self-talk is like gravity. What you attract is determined by the weight of your thoughts and where they are centred.
- Put self-belief at the centre of your thoughts.
- The warrior mental intervention package is about bringing the pillars of esteem, thoughts, feelings and words into alignment to support your goals and successes.
- Nurture your inner garden and it will blossom with inspiration, creativity and imagination.
- Your subconscious cannot differentiate between fantasy and reality.
- Charge yourself and your words with positive intention and the world will respond in kind.
- Create a mind movie by writing yourself a limitless script. Cast yourself as the hero, the best possible version of you.
- What you believe you become.

Chapter Fifteen // Gratitude

Thinking it is time to be grateful once you have peace, strength and abundance is akin to thinking it is time for someone with a luxury yacht to amass wealth. Waiting for success before expressing gratitude is putting the cart before the horse. Gratitude is the very doorway through which contentment and accomplishment make their entrance.

Gratitude is the foundation of life. It is part and parcel of the attitude of success. Foster this attitude of gratitude in each and everything you do. Make it a part of you. Build it into your thoughts, actions and plans. It is not enough to be grateful every now and then when something outstanding comes your way. Being grateful is an essential component in stepping off the wheel of stress-fuelled living and discovering the peace and strength available to you right now.

|| *'He that is of a merry heart*
hath a continuous feast' ||

Proverbs 15:15 The Authorised King James Holy Bible

However dark your world may feel, no matter how far away your dreams may seem, you have much to be grateful for. From the air you breathe, the food you eat and the words you read, through to your free will to step onto the path of the warrior, there are many, many things you can express gratitude for each and every day. An opportunity to learn is a reason for gratitude. Be grateful for the tough lessons, the insights learnt through trial and error as well as the wisdom gained through love and playfulness.

Make a list of all the things in your life you are grateful for. Be honest. Look deeply within yourself. Peel away the layers of anger and frustration until you find deep and authentic gratitude for everything that has delivered you breathing and kicking to this moment.

Create an affirmation of gratitude and say it each morning. For example: 'I am grateful for the success and abundance this day brings.' As you say it allow every cell in your body to greet the day in thanks. Breathe in through your nose to the base of your stomach. Feel your breath move through your body and rejoice in the gift of another day. Every time you repeat this exercise you acknowledge your existence as a gift. This acknowledgement will grow and nurture a garden of gratitude that will blossom with love. Love knows no boundaries.

Through this exercise, you come to the crossroads of each day without limits, ready to draw abundance and success into your world through the magic of grace. Express your gratitude throughout each day with your smile, eyes and body language.

|| *A warrior is grateful for battle as each challenge is a deep learning experience.* ||

Gratitude is the warrior's armour. It will protect you when you require it. Any time fear or stress stirs within you, step into gratitude. See it as a shield or force field protecting you from negativity and worry. It is almost impossible to worry about defeat when you are grateful for an opportunity to give something a go.

It is easy to see how this attitude magnifies success. Once you step out into the world grateful for the opportunity of life, fear falls away. Without the worry over not living up to false expectation or unrealistic ideals of perfection at all cost, you have a head start. When you are in this space you will be able to respond to any situation with an unclouded mind and sound reasoning. This is living in grace.

Identifying what you are grateful for will help you keep sight of what is most important in life. In the absence of gratitude we risk missing out on so much of what life has to offer. Beaming out an attitude of gratitude will attract abundance in the same way a lighthouse guides boats safely into harbour.

Being grateful for the simple things in life, such as the sun on your face, a shooting star on a cloudless night or the salty spray of the ocean, will bring you to life – body, mind and spirit. This kind of energy is attractive and dynamic. Like a child dashing across a field there is something contagious about someone who is truly alive. When you take the time to breathe in the beauty and majesty of the world around you that beauty and majesty becomes a living part of who you are. If you live constantly in a state of gratitude you will always have things to be grateful for. It is that simple.

Your ability to wonder and see possibility is proportionate to the level in which you embrace gratitude. The more grateful you become, the more beauty you will see. You will not just see the beauty that exists, you will see the beauty that could be. You will be able to see potential the average person cannot. Here lies the link between gratitude and the vision of an entrepreneur. This is a real secret of abundance and success.

The idea that we must fight and scratch our way to the top is a myth. The large body of allegory suggesting that empathy is for the weak is nothing but an outmoded fairy-tale. The cold and unscrupulous beings who claw their way through the ranks without a thought for the downtrodden are not the success-makers of the twenty-first century. Relying on such tactics is like an athlete relying on performance-enhancing substances to get to the Olympics. You are going to be found out and no one likes a cheat. Staking a claim to success based on the narcissistic idea that you deserve it more than someone else is setting yourself up for misery.

Winning at all costs is not winning at all. How can you be truly grateful for something you have gained through lies or coercion? You simply cannot. This kind of strategy robs people of the real joys in life. It also gives people a handicap. Manipulation, power play and conniving take up a lot of precious energy; this is working harder for less.

Putting your resources into building a network of support and respect is working smarter. Taking the time to see people and what they have to offer will put you at the head of your game. Never underestimate the potential of your colleagues. Treating everyone with respect will save you from future awkwardness. Your most inexperienced employee could be your boss one day.

It is more energy efficient to float to the top on the waves of gratitude than to struggle to the top against a current of opposition. Managers who leave ill feelings in their wake are focused only on short-term gain. These methods are for the untalented who do not believe they have what it takes to get places on their own merit. The effort of covering up and dismissing the accusations or disrespect of others will eventually take its toll. On the other hand, putting the same energy into developing effective communication, management skills and positive relationships will take you further without the hidden cost.

Aside from that, who do you want to wake up with each morning? Someone who is disconnected from the people they boss around each day? Or a warrior who is respected, trusted and championed by those they work with?

Express your gratitude to your co-workers. People thrive on being appreciated. You will get better results now and in the future if you acknowledge the ideas and strengths of others. Rather than being in competition with colleagues, the warrior creates a community of cooperation. As a warrior, you will be well-noted as a natural motivator who inspires great results. This is a more rewarding life than the micromanager or authoritarian will ever know.

The warrior is compassionate without being attached. Yes, this is possible. You are not forever beholden to the job, the career or the mentor you have now. When you affirm or write 'I am grateful for my job' in your journal do not attach who you are to that job. If you are attached your ability to grow and develop is limited. Also, inspiring and caring about your colleagues is different to being responsible for them.

Connecting to people and opportunities through gratitude keeps you in the here and now. Gratitude is for today. It recognises that everything is fleeting. Things can be taken away and there will also come a time when you may be ready to move on.

Gratitude is a real treasure in this stress-fuelled world. It is not the pot of gold but the rainbow that colours our world. It is all too easy to focus on the peace, strength and abundance the pot of gold will bring, but the real beauty is in the rainbow. Gratitude can transform routine into joy and ordinary opportunities into blessings. The pathway of success and abundance is open to you. It all starts and ends with gratitude.

- Peace, strength and abundance will enter your life through gratitude.
- Gratitude grows and nurtures the warrior within.
- Be grateful for everything that has brought you to this crossroads in life.
- Gratitude is a super power that will make you impervious to stress.
- Living through gratitude is investing in a joyful now and a joyful future.
- Gratitude is energy efficient.
- The journey of success begins and ends with gratitude.

Chapter Sixteen **//** # Abundance

Your abundant life begins with perception. Many people make the mistake of measuring abundance by the state of their bank balance; however, as it is a state of mind it is not so easily measured. Money may come and go like the tides, but abundance is perpetual in the warrior's heart and mind. So, you can stop wasting your time searching for it because you already have it.

An asset pool is merely an indicator of someone's wealth. In the modern world people can make or lose a fortune practically overnight. There are many business people who have made a fortune, lost a fortune, and gone onto make an even bigger fortune. These people know the real secret to abundance has little to do with money and everything to do with perspective.

Regardless of your current financial status I want you to switch on immediately to your abundance. Connect to the limitless you and infuse your thinking with belief and confidence. At every moment of your day you are at a crossroads with infinite possibilities available to you. Knowing this, believing in yourself and connecting to the limitless universe, is all you need to access abundance.

The inner resources you need to make dynamic transitions are always available to you. If you need a creative solution, guess what, you have an abundance of creativity. There is no limit to the number of creative solutions you can come up with in a day, a week, or lifetime.

The same applies to strategy. No one is ticking off the number of wealth-building strategies you have used. There is no quota on the number of auditions, interviews or consultations you can turn up to. The other good news is that having a single good idea improves the chances of you having many, many more. Coincidentally, there is also a limitless supply of positive thinking and energy at your disposal.

Believe in yourself and your ability and power to transform your world for the better, and other people will believe it too. It's all up to you. Transforming the way you see the world is not so hard once you give it a try. Change your perception about just one thing and you have started the habit of turning detrimental thinking into the empowering, positive mindset of a warrior.

|| *An abundant heart creates an abundant life.* ||

Being in a state of abundance is about saying goodbye to your ego and saying hello to the endless possibilities of expansion. Becoming abundant means overcoming the ego voice that will point to your failures and stamp your character with limiting labels. Once you label yourself as 'something' you become boxed into a reality. Your ego feels that finite reality is a safe place, but it is a false belief about a false reality.

You are welcome to step into abundance. It is not the exclusive club your ego wants you to think it is. The limitless you allows mistakes to be made and knows that there is no last chance. There is always a next time. The universe never gives up on you and nor should you. Life is not about how much you get knocked down. It is about how many times you get up again, and there is no limit to the number of times you can get back up. On the contrary, there is an abundance of energy available to you, so recharge, review and refocus – but never give up.

Abundance is infinite and your mindset, emotions and actions should reflect this. The number one rule of abundance is to see the world as infinite and your life as a series of possibilities. Think, feel and act as if there are countless opportunities ahead of you, and you will have it. Once you know this, you will naturally enter a state of external prosperity that mirrors your spiritually prosperous inner reality.

You are naturally abundant. You were born with a sense of love, happiness and contentedness that is akin to having an abundant mindset. So entering abundance is a return to who you are, free of the many learnt, limiting responses to the world. As a baby you reached out for what you wanted. You didn't stop to wonder about failure nor did you know fear or think that you might not deserve something. These are learnt ideas and it is time to unlearn them.

How *high* do you think? Take your soul out of your body, project it up and look down on your current thoughts. From this helicopter view make the decision to love who you are, inside and out. Elevated thoughts create elevated results.

Imagine yourself at the controls of a plane. As you fly through the sky a large cloud of fog suddenly surrounds the aircraft. As a pilot you are trained not to get caught up in the fog. Focus on what lies beyond the fog and you will make it through. Your fog may be bills, health, or a run of bad luck. Whatever it is, look beyond it to success. The fog is temporary. Set your uplifting attitude and energy to high.

Remind yourself that you are connected to all things. There is an abundance of resources available to you at any time. Take a moment to plug into possibility when you need a creative edge, solution or a new way of looking at things. You will be amazed at how contagious and addictive abundant thinking can be. Once you plug in you will find your energy reserves soar. There will be an electricity about you as people pick up on the field of possibility surrounding you.

The greatest machines on earth won't produce anything if they are not plugged into the right power source. You are and always have been capable of manifesting the life of your dreams. It is all just a matter of plugging into the source of abundance. That source is the mindset of the warrior: limitless, visionary and awakening.

- You are already absolutely and infinitely abundant.
- Fortunes may come and go, but abundance is perpetual.
- You are always at a crossroads of infinite possibility. Know this, believe in yourself, and abundance is yours.
- There are no limits on amazing ideas, creative solutions or positive thoughts. Have as many as you want!
- Having one fantastic idea exponentially increases the odds of you having many, many more.
- Setbacks are temporary. There is always another chance for success.

- Elevated thoughts create elevated results.
- Plug into the warrior mindset and charge up your field of possibility.
- Affirm out loud: 'I am a limitless, visionary and abundant warrior!'

Chapter Seventeen **//** Entourage

The people you spend the most time with have the most influence on who you become. The people in your everyday life are your teachers. The way they greet you, respond to your views and communicate with you contributes to your sense of identity and belonging. It would be great if all our friends and family jumped on board and supported our hopes and dreams with absolute passion. However, this is rarely going to happen and I am not sure it would be that helpful.

Everyone has a friend or family member who discourages personal growth and seems to do their best to suck the possibilities out of life. That's okay in small doses. However, if this sounds like all or most of your peer group have a think about the impact spending time in a limiting environment is having on you.

Negative thinking and pessimism is highly contagious. It takes courage to follow a dream when everyone around you is telling you it can't be done. More importantly, when you hit a bump in the road – and you will hit more than one – having someone around to push you back on track is invaluable. Whatever you do, when you face a challenge or hit an unexpected road block do not go to someone who is going to say, 'I told you it couldn't be done.'

Depressive thoughts can come from the workplace, magazines, the news, radio, movies or the Internet. Comparing yourself with unrealistic Hollywood ideals or barraging your mind with images of violence, depravity, and storylines of greed and manipulation will not help you on your path to greatness. The company you keep includes more than just the people you interact with. The books you read, the paintings on your wall, the games you play, all impress themselves into your thinking. You cannot choose your family, but you sure can choose the movies you watch and the music you listen to. Choose to mingle with the masters in art, literature and motivation.

> *'The key is to keep company only with people who uplift you, whose presence calls forth your best.'*
>
> Epictetus

To live in greatness surround yourself with inspiring people. If you live with negativity, or surround yourself with people who make poor choices and create constant trouble for themselves it is only a matter of time before you are pulled in by association. The way the human mind is wired makes us susceptible to losing our personal identity amidst a crowd of influence. Marketing companies use this vulnerability to their advantage. You can use the same knowledge to your advantage by surrounding yourself with great minds and spirits.

Many people believe they have a set place in the world or a limit on what they can achieve. This may be because of their childhood environment. It is not for other people to determine your capabilities. Only you can make that decision. You are the creator of your world. Your role in this lifetime is to create a reality where you can shine to your fullest potential. It is no one's responsibility but your own.

When you are presented with constant evidence of your limitations it is hard not to believe them. However, you now have the opportunity to turn all that around and know the biggest thing separating you from your vision is your belief. When you read inspirational biographies, or tales of everyday people overcoming hardship despite all odds you are presenting your mind with new evidence. You are showing yourself that there is another way. When you read of someone else's achievements take the journey of success with them. In this way you are driving the point home to your subconscious mind: success is open to everyone.

Success is natural; it is your belief that gets in the way. You were born as a perfect being. Only your perception keeps you from realising you are just as perfect today. Take ownership of your destiny by stepping into your dual role of master and magician.

Say it out loud:

Success is open to me now.
I will walk my path as the best version of me.
I write my own script and I choose success.

Your entourage includes your mentor, teachers, friends, family and colleagues. Even if you feel you are surrounded by negativity at home and work you can create a pocket of positivity for yourself. Taking up private lessons with a supportive teacher can help you accept encouragement from others. Your teachers and your mentor can coach you through obstacles and celebrate your successes with you.

Don't race off and quit your job because it is negative and destructive. Decide what you want to do and wait for the right time to make your dynamic transition. You cannot appreciate the good life until you have experienced the other side. If you've seen tough times use this to enhance your gratitude for the wonderful life you are now embracing.

As for the people in your life who quash your vision or discourage change, how are they faring? Are they wealthy, wise and wonderfully happy? Be grateful to them as they have shown you what negative thinking and not daring to make a change will get you. Look at the negative thinkers and ask yourself, 'What have I got to lose?'

Think about the entourage you would like to have. Have you ever asked the question, 'Who would I like to be stranded on a desert island with?' This is a little bit like that, without the island or the desert. There are no limits to this reality. The key here is to dream big. If your ambition is to be a great author your entourage may include interesting characters, insightful philosophers and inspiriting wordsmiths. What you don't need is someone tagging along saying you'll never get published or you are wasting your time.

You need the resilience to come away from disheartening encounters knowing that any criticism encountered is a reflection of the critic, not of you. You may also need the courage to distance yourself from anyone overly negative or outright abusive. You may even need to cut people from your life altogether. If you feel this is true for you, let people know that you will not accept their criticism. This will take strength and resolve, but it is important to stand your ground and set boundaries. Let the person know their negativity will not be tolerated and if they continue with derogative behaviour you will have no choice but to take a break from the relationship. Some relationships can take up so much time and energy with worry, guilt or heartache. It is hard, but you won't know yourself once you are free from a toxic connection. Losing you may even prompt the other party to change their ways. You could be doing more than yourself a favour.

> *'Associate with men of good quality if you esteem your own reputation; for it is better to be alone than in bad company.'*
>
> George Washington

No matter how uniquely talented or ambitious you are, you will not move forward without a supportive entourage. The president of a country has a team of advisors to help them gather information and make strong decisions. A Formula One driver is nothing without his entourage. There is not a single successful person on the planet who does not have a team helping them bring things together. You will not make it on this journey alone. Even if you don't believe the people you know are likely to be on your team, let them in on your dreams. Let them know what you are doing and keep them updated on your progress. You will find supporters in the most unexpected corners of your life.

Tell everyone! When you open your new bank account let the teller know you are starting an exciting new business. Ask the librarian about motivational authors or inspiring biographies. Take every opportunity to strike up a conversation and invite people into your dream. A few encouraging words from a stranger could lead to much more. This is all part of opening doorways to the new world you desire.

As you read this book, absorb the information and do the exercises. You are becoming the writer, director and hero of your story. Who do you want beside you?

Choose your network very, very carefully. They will help to shape your future. Ask yourself if the people in your life support your ambition. They don't have to agree with everything you say, but they do need to believe you will succeed. Identify the people – or even just one person – you can count on to believe in you. This is the beginning of your entourage. From here you can begin to build your team of success. A team that plays together wins together, it is that simple!

Spending time in an environment that does not match your values and ambitions can have a detrimental effect. However, it can also provide the motivation to make the changes you are dreaming of. You are a product of your environment so take a look around you. Declutter, refresh and revitalise your space with motivational images. How you live, what you wear and how you communicate are all part of the success picture.

How you respond to your environment and the people you encounter is up to you. There are plenty of people out there ready to provide you with a living, breathing example of what not to do. You can learn so much by observing the outcomes of the choices of others. You can see the consequences of not pushing yourself forward, putting in the minimum effort, or accepting the limiting opinions of others – everywhere. Let this be a lesson on how not to live your life. Find people who are living your dream to provide the clues on how to live successfully.

The people in your entourage do not need to share your vision. They can have their own goals and dreams. However, it is important to be with people who respect your values and boundaries and support your vision. If these areas are constantly being disrupted or disrespected it will channel your energy away from your vision and intention.

The most stoic of characters in the most challenging situations find their entourage within. They can recall a quote, book passage, mantra or a conversation that will get them through. However, that kind of endurance will drain your resources over time. It is far easier to change your environment and entourage than to pit yourself against spiritual detractors, day in, day out. To live in a healthy environment surrounded by supportive, thought-provoking people is a dream in itself. When you have this you can sail through any challenge life throws at you.

Through my experience, most people's circle of family and friends come with an aspect of fear and worry. Constant anxiety and drama within your entourage doesn't help anyone move forward. However, you have the power to change from this point onwards. When you change your thinking and dare to act on your dreams you will also be inspiring everyone you encounter.

Imagine the people in your entourage right now seeing you step off the carousel and live a fuller life. Sure, some of them might want you to get right back on the merry-go-round; but, there will be those excited by the possibilities opened to them. You will be their hero, so guide them well. Set a wonderful example of what living is all about for everyone in your past, present and future.

Life is for living, and experiencing and invoking the best in yourself and the people around you. Reading this book will engage the warrior within and activate your purpose. Align your thoughts, words, actions, feelings and entourage, and you will be limitless.

- The people and environment you spend time with influence your journey.
- Attitude is contagious.
- To live in greatness, surround yourself with greatness.
- Only you can determine your capabilities.
- Celebrate the success of others. Show your subconscious that success is everywhere and open to everyone.
- Your entourage includes your mentors, teachers, friends, family, colleagues, work environment, wardrobe and personal space. Create an entourage that will support and encourage your vision.
- Choose your companions carefully. You'll be counting on them.
- Show others that success is accessible. Be the hero. Live your dreams.

Chapter Eighteen **//** # Mentorship

The concept of mentoring dates back to Ancient Greece. When Odysseus embarked on the long journey to Troy he entrusted his realm into the care of his good friend, Mentor. When Athena wanted to give Odysseus advice during his twenty-year absence, and on his return to Ithaca, she chose to take the physical form of Mentor. We can presume that Athena chose this form because Mentor was such a trusted, wise and loyal friend. Indeed, Mentor's character was such that even the King of Ithaca heeded his advice.

A mentor is the most vital member of the warrior's entourage. Embarking on a quest for self-improvement means being open to new information, philosophies and strategies. Choosing a mentor can help you sort through the influx of material and make strong, definite decisions that are yours and yours alone.

Think of your mentor as the head coach in your game of life. The coach of a football team helps each player build on and take advantage of their strengths. They help the team recognise and tackle their weaknesses and to get their heads in the game. However, it is up to each individual to play the game. The coach can give direction and encourage reflection on what went well and what to do differently next time, but he doesn't play the game for you. This is a person you celebrate your successes with, but they scrutinise your performance and push you to be your very best.

Too many approaches can push and tug you in different directions making it hard to commit to a course of action. This is why choosing a single mentor for each stage of your journey can quicken your progress. When choosing a mentor look for someone with an outlook on life that is in harmony with your vision. Just like Odysseus, you want someone who can offer you wise and honest counsel. This is not another player on the field, but someone who stands outside the game. You are not looking for someone to compete with, you are looking for objectivity and experience.

You can find a mentor in the most unexpected places. I did not expect to be challenged to greatness in the pizzeria. In Frank, I found a wisdom and honesty that rang true to my purpose and spirit. I was willing to listen and be inspired by him. If I had disrespected him as a man I would never have benefitted from his guidance. So when you accept a mentor into your life it is important to be in the right headspace and to respect the process as well as the teacher.

If you want to be a singer you might find a mentor in your vocal coach. Ideally, you would be learning from someone who could inspire you to practise, train up and develop your talents, to help you find new range and introduce you to new techniques. For you to accept a teacher as a mentor you would devote yourself to their process and focus purely on their methods. A teacher should know what your goals are so you are both working towards the same outcomes.

A mentor will put new goals ahead of you and push you to achieve them. You will feel that your mentor sees through your insecurities and unpolished ability to the outstanding performer that lies within. They will be committed to setting your talents free, just as you are committed to trusting your mentor can set them free.

A mentor will take you outside your everyday thought process. It is their role to ensure you are continually growing, not just in a particular skill set but in confidence and emotional intelligence. You are looking for someone you can trust enough to open up to. The process of opening up and addressing your concerns and fragilities will see you blossom into limitlessness. With your mentor you can knock down any boundaries and feel a whole new person emerge within.

However, you must be committed to the process. There is no point to fighting with the methods of your mentor. When feedback is offered take it with humility. There is no room for defensiveness in this relationship. You must trust that anything your mentor says is coming from a place of honour. So, it is important to consciously choose them with care.

Take a break and list the people you think could be your mentor starting from tomorrow. Is there one person you know who will take the time to listen to your dreams, see your greatest potential and push you to succeed against the odds? Who will challenge your thinking, scoff at your excuses and re-invoke your passion? Most importantly, who do you trust enough to share your ultimate dreams with as well your insecurities and doubts? If you know one person who fits the bill you are a very lucky individual.

If you can't think of anyone, put the call out to the universe. Be on the lookout for signs. Look inwards for guidance to direct you to the right person for this time in your life. If you are not already clear of your vision and intentions set them out now. Otherwise, meditate on finding a mentor in your morning contemplation. Sit quietly and send it out into the universe. I can assure you that someone will come your way. Chances are there is already someone in your life ready to motivate and challenge you to better things. It is the old adage: once you are ready to learn the mentor appears.

Prepare yourself to be the perfect mentee by listening to others, being open to critique and developing self-disciplinary skills. Being a great student will help you attract a great mentor. Trust that the universe has heard your call and you have been taken care of.

This does not mean you should sign up to the first person who comes along. Be discerning and check in with your intuition before you hand over your absolute trust to anyone. Take your time and wait for the person you are looking for. You will know them.

Once you have found your mentor tell them very specifically what your intentions are. Ask them how they can help you achieve your goals. This is a turning point in any warrior's journey. Taking the humble position of student as your mentor shines their light on your path will allow you to see the obstacles ahead. You can identify the obstacles to be avoided and how to tackle the rest effectively. Think of your mentor as the lighthouse that shines a light across the sea of dreams, guiding you safely to your intentions, goals and desires.

Once you have found your mentor it is very important you commit to their teachings. When the going gets tough and they are pushing you out of your comfort zone it is this commitment that will get you through. To help you through discomfort and challenges, and when they tell you things you just don't want to hear, write them a commitment letter. Open your diary and pledge yourself to your mentor in ink.

Here is an example:

Dear Mentor,

I commit to listening to everything you say, to following your direction and taking heed of your counsel. I promise to bring an open heart and ready mind into your presence.

Sign and date your statement. You may wish to give your mentor a copy to acknowledge it as an exchange of love and commitment. Your mentor wants to see you grow and you also want to grow. As student and teacher, you have a shared goal and a mutual vision, and you will cooperate to build the future of your dreams. The right mentor will make a significant impact on your everyday life for a stage of your journey.

Yes, you have made a commitment to your mentor, but there will come a time when you outgrow them. A mentor will come into your life, take you to the next harbour and move you on. Many teachers will recognise when their student is ready to move to the next level. They may even recommend or introduce you to someone who can take your further. When I have a mentor I do not aim to be like them or even as good as them. I always strive to become a better me under their tutelage. Once I feel I have reached the limits of our student/mentor relationship it is time to move on. Every great teacher wants to see their students outdo them, and there is no better way to honour your teacher than to better them.

Life has a funny way of indicating when it is time for a change. You will be presented with new philosophies, networks and ideas that push you outside the scope of your mentor. I can tell you from experience that when the time comes to move on and find a new mentor it will be obvious to both of you.

You can also be mentored by a book, in a discussion group, or through any experience that challenges you to grow or pushes you outside your comfort zone. This is where people get lost; they think they don't have a mentor. A mentor is simply a personal development tool.

A warrior uses many different tools and strategies as they strive forwards to great accomplishment. They may use a 'sword' to break through barriers, a 'shield' for protection and a 'cape of courage' to empower them across the boardroom. A mentor is a part of the warrior's toolkit. I use this terminology with absolute respect. It is also with respect that you must recognise the time to move onto a new mentor so you can take on new challenges.

Without challenge there is no growth. Once your mentor is no longer challenging you it is time for a change. Accept this and find someone who will push you harder. This is part of the process. If you want to grow into an incredible and inspiring individual then you will be up to the challenge.

- Your mentor is the head coach in your game of life, but it is up to you to play the game.
- Too many paths can lead you nowhere. Commit to a mentor to quicken your progress.
- You may find your mentor in an unexpected way. Wisdom exists outside of expectation.

- To find a great teacher, be a great student.
- A mentor will challenge and push you out of your comfort zone and into greatness.
- That which challenges you teaches you. You can be mentored through a book, a discussion or an experience.
- Do not strive to be like your mentor but to become great through their tutelage. A great teacher will want you to outgrow them.
- When your mentor is challenging you and you just want to quit, stick with it. When you feel comfortable and at ease with your lessons, move on.

Chapter Nineteen **//** # Spirit

Picture a horse in a field strewn with autumn leaves. The breeze comes up reminding every inch of the paddock it is part of a living universe. The horse pounds through the leaves, stirring them towards the heavens in a dance of its own delight. Close your eyes and imagine the horse as a channel for the life force that rises up through the ground to catch a ride with the wind. The very earth lurches with the need for adventure and the dust in the air glories at the excitement of new things ahead.

Breathe in the sounds, smells, colours and soft warmth of this golden afternoon. Catch the breeze upon your face and taste the static in the air. Lose yourself in the image and connect with the spirit of the moment. Bond with the spirit within you. Let it move you. Give yourself permission to release the catch on the gate or to smash down the wall. Let it flow and fill you. Let it overflow and expand out into the universe.

It takes such a lot of effort to keep your spirit harnessed when the wind is full of possibility and the ground you walk on is alive with adventure. Release the last hold on your spirit and delight in a dance of your own creation.

A high-spirited horse is one that is proud and unbroken. It is hard not to stand in awe of the beauty and majesty of such a creature. Unleash your spirit and you will know the glory of living in peace, strength and abundance. It is an electric state of being that will charge your environment with potential. When you plug into this space you will feel excitement in the air as if something is about to happen. This anticipation is your spirit savouring the possibilities around and within you. The potential locked in every moment of your day is immeasurable. It awaits your invitation – go on, set it free!

Your spirit has a reason for being. Its strength of purpose gives it an electrifying enthusiasm for everything that comes your way. It is overjoyed at the opportunities that life brings. Your spirit knows nothing of fear; it is here to experience all it can. It is an unlimited, expansive and endlessly abundant force housed within. You can recognise a fellow warrior by the gleam in their eyes as the fire in their soul flickers into the open world.

With all this talk of enthusiasm and energy you might mistake hyperactivity for high spirits. Having high spirits is not about being the loudest person in the room or dominating every conversation. It is about being plugged into the environment and working with the potential of every moment with the highest of intention. A cat poised silently and attentively is just as spirited as a playful kitten. The person in the room demanding to be front, centre and heard is missing the point and, in most cases, missing the potential in front of them. This is because they are disconnected.

Commune with your soul and ask for guidance and signs. You will see things that inspire you to action and encourage you to live. However, going within is not enough. You must also connect to the world around you. You are the bridge between life and spirit. Be the life and soul of your own party. Get into the spirit of things and electrify your world.

When you get into the spirit of a situation you connect with its possibilities. High spirits are contagious, but to lift the energy of those around you it is important to empathise with their current energy. Tuning into the vibrations and actually feeling your surroundings is how true connections are made. When you actively link to the spirit of those you meet you are freeing something inside them. You are meeting with them as an equal. This is a very powerful attribute to have. It ensures you are remembered, and you will quickly build an entourage of spirited people with similar values.

Being high in spirit does not put someone above or below anyone else. High-spirited people are of this world. They make meaningful connections with others as they adventure through life. They do not always make the best decisions and can suffer over trivialities. They can plunge into despair and have moments when they feel unworthy or incapable of growth. However, the call to life is so powerful and addictive they won't stay down for long. From inside the well it takes only the glimpse of a butterfly hovering overhead to revitalise hope and restore the vision of a dynamic future.

|| *'That is why they are warriors* ||
of light. Because they make
mistakes. Because they ask
themselves questions. Because

|| *they are looking for a reason* ||
– and are sure to find it.'

Paulo Coelho

Your feelings are like invitations. You will attract people and situations into your life that synchronise with your feelings. This is why it is so important to check in with your spirit daily. If you find something weighing on your spirit, or pressing on your conscience, your best course of action is to address the issue head on. This will keep your spirit light and free. Over time, a habit of ignoring issues or hoping they will just go away will burden your spirit with 'dis-ease'. How can you be free and connected when your spirit is heavy with regret or anger?

Even if you cannot address a situation or a person directly, spend time contemplating your involvement, reactions and feelings so you can move forward, light in the knowledge you have learnt all you can from the scenario. Your spirit is here to learn, so it won't be held back by negative developments as long you are committed to exploring your feelings and facing up to who you are. You are in the on-going process of getting to know yourself better.

People work on their bodies and their minds. They run, swim, go to the gym, read and strategise. But, how much time do we spend improving our spirit? Working on what is within is an essential part of improving that which is without. You do not need to train your spirit as it is already a vital and perfect force. However, you do need to pay attention to the psyche that houses it. If you let too much clutter and doubt build up around the doorways it will hold your spirit in check. If something is not done to clear the way your spirit can become trapped inside. It will wilt away like a plant without the sunshine. But, even after years of darkness a seed can burst into life once the sun starts to shine, so it is never too late.

Training your spirit is a matter of expanding your boundaries and knowing it is safe to soar. Letting your spirit stretch its wings will ensure it cannot forget how to fly. It may be a little rusty and unsure at first so give it plenty of room to build its confidence. Develop a training regime for your spirit. This will involve communicating with your soul and making meaningful connections between your inner castle and the outside world.

You are in the process of integrating your mind, body and spirit so that nothing is separating you from the wisdom within. The wisest mentor imaginable is already a part of you. You are on a journey to find that sage. When you are inspirited you can find truth, love and wisdom in every situation. With time and practice you will see that they are with you always. Let your spirit be like an electrical current connecting you to the world around you. Shine brightly for all to see.

It is so refreshing to be in a room with people who are alive and flowing with a spirited current. Your ego may find the idea of being in a room of vibrant, confident people daunting. However, it is a comforting and reassuring setting that makes you feel at home. There is a relaxed authenticity about people who have switched onto spirit.

When you become aware of your inner glow you will see yourself differently. The way you perceive yourself is how you project yourself to the outside world. Therefore, I urge you to look within and awaken the fire in your soul so you can see yourself shine like a diamond.

- Your spirit rejoices at the opportunity to live.
- You are the vehicle for your spirit. Set your spirit free and you will be fuelled by its enthusiasm and limitless energy.
- Being of high spirits makes you equal to everyone else.
- Your feelings are invitations to draw people and situations into your reality.
- Your spirit knows nothing of fear or judgment. It wants to learn all it can about the world.
- Negative developments won't hold your spirit back; unresolved issues will.
- The warrior seeks to integrate mind, body and spirit. This is a journey to wholeness.
- Be in the spirit of things and you will see potential everywhere.

Part Three

Stories from the Super Side //

Chapter Twenty **// Adding the Extra
to Ordinary**

This final chapter is dedicated to and written by those who have already experienced the warrior's way. I know how powerful awakening the inner warrior has been for me, but what inspired me to write the book was the change I have witnessed in others. The following is a sample of the feedback I have received from people who have chosen to enliven their spirit within by awakening their inner warrior. The strength, peace and abundance I have found is open to you right now. You just have to believe it and so I share these stories as testimony to the warrior's way. Don't dream it – breathe into it, believe it and be it.

Wow Jacob! What a difference a day and a session with you can make. Yesterday after our meeting, I got on the bus and had a good chat with myself. There was another guy having a chat with himself too, however I suspect that had more to do with mental illness than love, gratitude and surrender.

Anyway, I started to think about what you had said about our living circumstances and I felt such positive energy and a strong sense of optimism, even though it was pouring with rain. For the next hour I floated through the traffic, the crowded bus, the noise and red lights as if I was the richest man in the world without a care in the world. I picked up our children from school and hugged them and listened carefully to their day as we made our way home.

As we entered the house I received a phone call from the real estate agent asking if they could come down and look at the water damage the rain had brought. I could hear trepidation and tiredness in the agent's voice. When she arrived I welcomed her in and watched as she walked throughout the house appearing more uncomfortable seeing the water damage everywhere. I watched her as she looked around and saw all the makeshift accommodation, beds on the lounge and the cupboards, tables moved and displaced in each room. She apologised to me and I said, 'it's not your fault.'

She said we need to fix this for good and I said, 'Thank you for looking after us'. She asked me if the kids were okay and I said, 'They are thrilled – it's like camping for them.' I added, 'you must be exhausted – I imagine there are lots of people with water problems.' She thanked me for understanding. I smiled at her with genuine empathy. My daughter offered her a cup of tea.

The agent inspected the whole house with me and even climbed up onto the roof to look at the damage. She rang a contractor who turned up with industrial fans while she was still here. Jacob we still have water damage but we no longer have any problems.

After she left we went out to have dinner. It continued to pour with rain as we walked from the car park. I held an umbrella above my son's head and hugged him close. I watched my wife do the same with our daughter. We enjoyed dinner and I apologised for my recent mood. They all accepted my apology. I told them I needed their help. I asked and they all said yes.

I said that I needed to understand how everyone felt about how we were living and if they wanted to move or stay. I asked everyone to speak and they did. They shared their feelings and I remained quiet and just listened. They all said they wanted to stay in this house and that they are happy. We then started to speak about what we would like a home to represent instead of focusing on a house's problems or limitations. I was subtle but it has started to change everything.

We talked about how we wanted to feel in our home. We talked about wanting to feel inspired and nurtured as we walk in – excited to be home and warm and re-energised. We are going to create a space that represents our family, our dreams, our vision and our creativity. We are going to create a home that other people want to be part of, where they want to come in good times and bad.

A place where the energy and laughter and love and passion is infectious. Where – despite the storms outside and the flooding and rain – there is a safe port where we can find beauty, wonder excitement. Where a leaky roof and cramped spaces won't stop us appreciating what is important, how to grow through adversity, how to hold tight to our dreams, how to make those dreams reality, how to get better as things get harder, how to tap into potential, how to discover our gifts, how to learn from each other and to build a better world.

Jacob, thank you for reminding me of what is important and that the change in the world and my world starts with me.

Andrew

Not only has Jacob been my mentor and friend, he has continuously inspired me to become better and achieve more. He has guided me into making wise and well calculated decisions. Over the years, he has been a significant and positive influence in my business and personal life. His authenticity and kind heart makes him one of a kind, because of this man I am where I am today, Jacob was my light in the dark.

Sam Bajis, Actor

Jacob showed me how to stretch myself, out of my comfort zone where everything was easy. He taught me that if you want your business to grow to the next level then as the business owner it is your obligation to extend yourself personally to the next level. Jacob showed me how to go within to achieve without, we did mind work, meditation, emotional intelligence, and the art of healing through conversations, it was an amazing life changing process.

Did I like it? NO.

Did I learn and grow from being mentored by Jacob? YES Thank you Warrior Jacob!

Cosimina Nesci (Personal & Corporate Image Brand Specialist)

Jacob, you have woken the inner warrior in me and my team and have helped lead us to success over the last 3 years. Your broad knowledge and understanding of people is testimony to why you have and will continue to be a success in your chosen field. The ability you have to light up a room and get people to listen, is a great gift and you use it to help those who want to bring on change and look for the support and guidance from yourself in getting there.

What can I say but you really made me understand the true meaning of WOW and what it should bring to my customers. You delivered one of the most inspirational workshops I have attended in a long time. Your understanding of people and how to get the most out of them is fantastic and very refreshing. The team are still buzzing and for a leader of people I could not have asked for more. The journey continues for us and with your help and guidance we will be the best we can be as we strive to be Number One! ONE TEAM, ONE DREAM!!!!!!

Keep up the great work my friend!

Salvatore Dema (Area Sales Manager – Victoria, BankWest)

Jacob Galea is one of the most entertaining and insightful regular guests on my radio show. He was so good I decided to take him on as a warrior coach to help push me in the right direction to achieve my goals in this cut throat world of radio and TV, I am now on the top of my game thanks to this man's knowledge and guidance, thankyou Corporate Warrior!

Mike Goldman (Award Winning Actor)

From the moment I met Jacob I was wowed and excited for the opportunity to work alongside him. When Jacob flew back to Sydney, I was left motivated, buzzing with enthusiasm to achieve and always do better. I was left mentally exhausted in a great way and filled with ideas and knowledge. I hope Jacob and I cross paths again in the future, Jacob has awoken something within me that has enabled me to be at the top of my game in this cut-throat corporate arena.

Adam L. (Business Development Manager)

I have known Jacob Galea for over 3 years now as a colleague through dealing with business clients for coaching and mentoring. On meeting Jacob there was an immediate connection and understanding that he could put people at ease and get them to talk freely and openly about any problems. By being able to quickly develop rapport with his clients, Jacob builds trust which provides an environment that is stress free and is able to get to the source of the issues. By focusing on the present he enables clients to be able to see the possible solutions and actions that they can take so that they can be in control of the situation and the outcomes.

Jacob has an approach that is supportive and inquiring and quickly gets to the real concerns that are driving the unwanted emotions and or behaviours. By understanding the thinking that created the roadblocks Jacobs clients are able to shift their attitudes and behaviours so that they can achieve the results that they want and need. I highly recommend Jacob to anybody who is looking to really achieve the most out of their life, whether it be personal, professional or in business.

Paul Mracek JP, MIEAust, CPEng, FAIM, GAICD
(CEO – Kotan Australia Pty Ltd)

To People who Aspire to be the Best they Can Be!

I've had the pleasure of knowing Jacob Galea the majority of his adult life. Having first met him when he began his journey through the martial arts. Then as a young student he possessed an enormous amount of disciple, energy, focus and intelligence. He had the capacity to focus his entire being into the moment and achieve such clarity in his movements. He rose through the ranks quickly and gained great respect amongst his peers. At the time he had begun an apprenticeship in the printing industry, but unbeknown to us all he had a very special path and purpose. Soon the student would became a master.

10 years later, Jacob found his true purpose in life, in the area of master motivator in the corporate business world. Using the same disciple, energy, focus and emotional intelligence. He is now applying his martial arts skill by mentoring and motivating some of Australia's most successful entrepreneurs. He has built a very successful business with an impressive list

of clients. He has achieved a high level of emotional intelligence and self-awareness, which are quite rare for someone who is so young. His life's work has led him to write a book which I strongly recommend to anyone who is interested in self-mastery and becoming the very best they can be.

I am proud and honoured to have been a witness to his remarkable journey and look forward to what the future lies for the young master.

Edward Cabello (Martial Arts Practitioner)

I can say this with my hands on my heart and deep purpose in my soul ... there are not many people I have met in the world that I believe can make "anything" happen.

Jacob Galea is one of these very rare people. And I have the pleasure to call him a great friend, a colleague, a mentor, a sounding board, and a spiritual conduit.

Jacob has been in my life for many years, and at no stage since we first met has his connectedness wavered or his sense of purpose strayed. His thirst for knowledge and understanding is no less intense, or his compassion for others any less enduring than from the first time we met.

His will to be authentic, stay authentic, and live a life of purpose is a will that I envy and respect. *I always have and I always will.* You see Jacob subscribes to the notion that he has a rightful place in this universe, and that if he is courageous enough and determined enough, that his "rightful place" will be presented – and his journey of service will continue and become clearer.

Jacob promotes beautiful narratives in a way which invoke the soul and uplift the spirit. His energy is both calm and vibrant at the same time ... but his will to support and nurture others is unquestionable.

Jacob is a self-proclaimed warrior. A wise warrior who is calm, considerate, thoughtful and self-aware. And most importantly a spiritual warrior who makes this world a better place, and easier to understand.

Gino

About the Author

Jacob Galea's journey has taken him from factory worker to success coach and mentor. He attributes his transformation to his ability to tap into his inner warrior and the power of the mind. Jacob believes everyone can access the wisdom that lies deep inside all of us.

As a trainer, Jacob has helped thousands of people and businesses all over the world to become limitless and live with purpose. He has shared his knowledge, wisdom, guidance, and secrets in front of huge audiences. Intrigued by the untapped ability of the mind, Jacob has studied and applied many techniques over the past twenty years including emotional intelligence, hypnotherapy, visualisation and art of war strategies. His powerful Warrior Training Program and Guidance System draws on this knowledge, personal insight and his hands-on experience.

A karate black belt champion, Jacob mixes Zen, leadership, mind coaching and inner transformation with his unshakeable belief in the human spirit to deliver a personal development system that works. He understands the power of thought and utilises skills honed through years of martial arts training to bring discipline, focus and clarity to the minds of corporate leaders. He also brings calm and clarity to stressed executives burdened by deadlines and overloaded schedules. An ability to identify and implement creative business strategies and his personal commitment to a winning process is a trademark of this inspirational entrepreneur. As a boardroom advisor and personal lifestyle coach, Jacob leads individuals, teams and organisations to become unstoppable, corporate warriors.

Jacob has been featured in BRW, The Sydney Morning Herald, The Sunday Telegraph, Good Weekend Magazine, Australian Institute of Management, Body and Soul, Mix 106.5FM radio, MX magazine and Blitz magazine and writes a monthly column in Ultra Fit magazine.

Jacob lives in Sydney Australia and can be contacted at jacob@jacobgalea.com or through www.jacobgalea.com. He looks forward to hearing your transformational stories.

"Life is about creating experiences that best serve your authenticity. It is time to do some deep soul searching and embark on an artistic journey to create a super life for a super you. This is an ongoing process where you are always seeking and learning new techniques to refine your craft and know yourself. Your life is a unique story – make it a super one!"

Jacob Galea